The Sacrifice

~ Other books from Morten Moore Publishing ~

Within This Covenant: Confession & Community in the Lord's Supper
by Eileen Moore

No Regrets: Caught in the Crossfire of an African Civil War
by Julia Vaughan

Jaybyrd: The Hermit of Sycamore Canyon
by Eileen Moore

The Sacrifice
by Ruth Mortenson

Published by
Morten Moore Publishing
Flagstaff, AZ

Book design and cover design: Morten Moore Publishing

Copyright held by Ken & Ruth Mortenson, 2018

ISBN 978-0-9991108-7-4

The
Sacrifice

Ruth Mortenson

Contents

The Question	1

Part I

The Gift of a Son	5
A Man Off to War	27
Arguing with God, Losing	43

Part II

Abraham: A Journey	55
The Covenant	59
Sarah	63
Hagar	73
Ishmael	77

Second Son	81
Cast Out	89
Isaac	99
Upon This Peak	109
By Faith	119

Part III

The Lessons We Must Learn	125
Confronting Grief	151
Walking By Faith	159

The Question

In Genesis, the first book of the Bible, chapter 22, we read the story of God testing a man, Abraham. This man was asked to offer his son as a sacrifice on a stone altar. Not only was he asked to offer Isaac as a sacrifice, he was to be the one wielding the knife and lighting the fire.

The story has come down through the centuries, laying the foundation for scholars to argue endlessly over one central question:

> *How could God ask a man to kill*
> *and offer his son as a sacrifice?*

This was the son who had been promised and anticipated through long decades, God's fulfillment of His promise. How could Abraham carry through on that request? How could he bind his son and plunge the knife into the thick arteries of his neck?

We read the story, knowing that God will halt the plunge of the knife, that he will stay Abraham's hand with a single word. We know the real sacrifice is already caught in the bushes nearby. And yet, for any parent, we shudder at the thought of being asked to sacrifice a child. We ask how Abraham could have been willing to commit this act.

How many parents down through the centuries have cradled the lifeless body of a child, screaming to the heavens one word? Why?

For that parent, this question is not theoretical. The grief rips at every inner fiber as a parent strains to understand how God could tear the one He loves from their very existence. Like many parents I faced that fear every day my son rode away from our home on his bike or explored some new venture. With some relief, I saw him reach age 18, thinking that childhood dangers were behind us. I could relax my vigilance just a bit.

And then one day, God asked,

Do you trust me?

Part I

"Brothers, we do not want you to be ignorant about those who fall asleep, or to grieve like the rest of men, who have no hope."

I Thessalonions 4:13

The Gift of a Son

To understand what it meant for us to trust God, to understand what it meant to give up our son, I would begin by taking you back to the day that Marty was born.

One moment I was sleeping soundly, the next moment amniotic fluid flooded the bed around my hips. We dropped off our daughter at a friend's house and drove to the hospital.

The staff at the hospital is trained to react calmly but after tucking me into bed, the desire to push overtook my body. I was within moments of delivering with the doctor no where in sight.

"Don't push!" the nurse screamed at me.

The doctor rushed into the roomwas there, shoving his hands into gloves, calling out orders. He glanced over the sheet at me and shrugged.

"I ran every stop sign on the way here. I've been up all night. I just got home when the nurse called me back to the hospital."

I smiled. "No cops, I hope."

"Nope. One more push and we got it."

Marty burst into the delivery room, announcing his

arrival with a loud cry. I strained upward to see the baby as they announced we had a boy.

There is something special about little boys who grub through the dirt or wave a stick through the air in an imaginary tale. I marveled over the little shorts and t-shirts in the boys section of the department store and imagined a little boy racing around the yard as I worked outside. I wanted a little boy in our growing family.

Through nine months of waiting for his arrival, I had begged God for a healthy little boy. As we cuddled together in the hours after his birth, I was delighted in the gift of this precious child. I loved this little boy.

When a mother brings her first child into the world, there are so many questions. We have no experience in birthing a child and tending to the baby's needs. Every parent works through the details of how and when to feed this tiny being. Where I struggled with my firstborn, now it seemed so natural to tip my nipple into Marty's mouth when he cried. We managed the umbilical cord and circumcision as it healed. Very quickly, we fell into a routine of feeding and diaper changing. He was easily sleeping six hours at night within a couple of months in his bassinet. When awake he was a quiet, happy baby, cooing at us as we marveled over his perfection.

Then, three months after his birth, I realized that I was pregnant again. I was not prepared to go through another pregnancy so soon. Months passed as my belly grew and I felt the first stirring of another child in my womb. Marty's younger sister was born just 360 days after Marty made his appearance.

When we arrived home, I carefully placed our new baby girl in her bassinet in our front room. The bassinet was low, with the edge only two feet above the floor. Marty watched my actions intently and then crawled toward the bassinet. He gripped the edge and pulled himself to a standing position to peer over the edge. With a big smile he began to pat the baby's back. His patting turned into hard thumps. We jumped forward to intervene in his heavy-handed affection. Laughing, I assured him he was a loving brother.

The next few months were difficult as I struggled to manage a newborn and a one year old who was not walking. My husband spent long hours in our business and my friends seemed a little impatient with my struggle. At 18 months, Marty took his first steps and I moved into a sprint to keep up with him. If he was too quiet, I learned to look at what new, creative hobby he had developed.

One evening, I heard my husband yell, "What are doing with my jogging shoes?"

Racing into the bathroom, I found Marty and his dad face to face over the toilet, the jogging shoes in the bowl. Marty had graduated from unrolling the toilet paper to washing dirty shoes in the toilet.

He could push a 40 pound bag of dog food to the floor, creating a pellet-fueled skating rink. While eating, he might fling his dish across the room, upsetting the mealtime routine.

We were becoming familiar with the perspective of a two-year-old. I might laugh over shoes in the toilet, at least they weren't mine, but torn books and broken toys left me frustrated over my inability to anticipate Marty's every move.

By the time Marty turned three, I was no longer laughing. His erratic behavior seemed to be beyond that of his peers. I asked an instructor at the local teacher's college to evaluate our son. He did not fail to disappoint them, refusing to stay in his chair long enough to complete any test. When I returned, they were unable to explain his challenging behavior but they did suggest that he needed to be kept occupied with directed activities. I resolved to become a super mom, directing my children's lives.

While I thought I would be the teacher, my son had much to teach me.

With school came new challenges. The length of Marty's attention span was short. His tendency to act in unexpected ways created a problem in the classroom. The teacher was responsible for twenty other children and could not focus on Marty alone. Marty learned very little that year. By April, his teacher was suggesting that we hold him back for another year of kindergarten. I had no intention of following his advice as his younger sister was right behind him.

Watching Marty play with other boys, I noticed that he often seemed detached. While a group of boys his age might all converge on a sand pile, pushing their trucks and hands through the sand to create roads and small jumps, Marty remained on the edge, lost in his own fantasy. His sisters, however, were not to be denied. They frequently found ways to involve him in their activities.

Serenity, his older sister, would tie the handle of our little red wagon onto the back of our bike. After securing her passengers, she would pedal down the street, giving them a ride. When Marty wished to pedal the bike while she rode, she would have nothing to do with such a plan.

"Mom, as reckless as Marty could be, do you think I was about to trust him to pull me?" she asked later. I had to agree that she had been wise in her assessment of the risk.

With his first grade teacher, the complaints grew about Marty's lack of attention and his ability to follow instructions. I promised to help Marty with his simple homework lessons at home. Yet, life at home could be somewhat chaotic as Marty burst from the confines of the classroom, anxious to recreate his fantasies outside. He barely shuffled into second grade.

By this time, the special education teachers had become aware that this was a child who needed extra help, but due to budget restraints and the strictures of certification, they could not easily add him to their schedules. Instead, Marty was introduced to rote lessons in sight reading. When a friend, with accreditation as a reading specialist, offered to work with him using phonetics, I desperately accepted her offer. She relished working with Marty as he eagerly responded to her one-on-one style, complete with special rewards for each small step of progress.

As he entered the third grade with his new reading skills, I was sure that the majority of our troubles in school were over. With dismay I learned that he was not completing his school work. His teacher insisted that he was not paying attention. As Marty arrived home, I would ask about homework and he would assure me that he had no homework. Another year rolled by as I struggled with the teachers and school administrators.

I began to talk about forming a support group for mothers with over-active boys, a time to vent and seek advice. I knew several mothers who needed such a group but we were all too busy running after our children.

Both his sisters were creative and smart, though his younger sister joined him in speech therapy. Unlike Marty, Molly had no problem completing her work. The teachers were fairly certain that his problems lay at home while I struggled to manage a busy schedule between home and business. Ken worked ten hours a day, adding an additional six hours on Saturdays.

Three weeks into the fourth grade, I was summoned to a parent-teacher conference. I was certain I was facing more complaints of inadequate performance. Far worse, I learned that the teacher was ejecting our son from his classroom, claiming that he refused to learn. This did not sound like Marty. When he was engaged, he was eager to learn. The teacher stated that Marty often stared out the window, disengaged from the activities in the classroom.

I bit my tongue against the angry words that formed in response to a teacher who seemed arrogant and uncaring. The counselor's next words stopped me cold.

"Ruth, we are placing Marty in a special-ed classroom."

What? Could they do that without my permission?

"We would like you to meet Dotty Haughton, the

teacher in this classroom."

I looked over at a short, stout woman, smiling at me. Utter rage rose to the surface as I struggled for control. How dare they presume to make decisions about my son without first talking to me? At the same time, I had to acknowledge I had failed to act effectively when the teacher had talked to me.

"So, how many hours a day would he be in this classroom?" I asked. "What about the rest of the school day?"

"Again, as we said, this is a special classroom. The students are with Mrs. Haughton the entire day. They go out to recess and to lunch with the other kids but she uses special techniques that help her students learn. Marty needs that special help."

"I don't want him isolated, kept away from the other students."

"We are not offering another choice."

Staring at the circle of impassive faces around me, I felt that I had been set up with this meeting. All the decisions had been made. I was simply there to agree to what they had decided.

Dotty Haughton asked me to come down to her classroom which was filled with posters, books, on-going experiments and special areas for each activity. She showed me a board with paper pockets, demonstrating how each student started the day with a set dollar amount in paper money. If they behave well, they accumulated the dollars throughout the week. The paper money was used in an auction of small toys and treats at the end of the day on Friday. Poor behavior could cause a student to lose a little *cash*. Working against my desire for our son to be considered normal, I was intrigued to see how this would appeal to Marty.

In the days that followed I quickly understood that Marty was functioning at a higher level than the other children in that classroom. I grew more angry with the manipulation of the school staff. Yet, I could see he was responding well to the reward system. Dotty and her aide, Brenda, quickly jumped on his failure to follow through when given instructions. His grades crept up.

Shortly after he had been removed from the fourth grade classroom, I had sought help from outside the school system to understand the learning issues Marty faced. I was directed to a neuro-psychologist who claimed he could identify the issues we were facing. Two weeks later, we learned that Marty was to be diagnosed with Attention Deficit Disorder.

This diagnosis became very popular in the years that followed. Many children were labeled with the initials ADD. As I researched Attention Deficit Disorder, I recognized my son's behavior fit the scale used for ADD. My husband and I shared a few of those symptoms though each of us had learned to compensate for our limitations. My husband refused to accept the label.

Ken began to help more at home, drilling Marty in his multiplication tables and math problems. Under his tutoring, Marty could quickly answer equations from the multiplication tables when quizzed in their evening sessions. The study sessions began to lag. Two weeks later, he asked Marty to give him an answer to the equation: 9 x 7= ___. Marty stared at him blankly, then insisted he had never heard this one before. Confronted by Marty's confusion, Ken began to understand the struggle within his son's brain.

The biggest challenges came as Marty acted impulsively without considering the consequences of what he was doing. He struggled to be organized and was often careless in completing a task. He was easily distracted, struggling to stay focused. Today, we know these are some of the most common symptoms of ADD, but for the teachers and the counselor at his school this was new territory. At times, Dotty seemed to be the only one who listened to my concerns.

I had hoped that by the end of the school year, Marty would be ready to return to a regular classroom. He remained with Dotty the following year. His grades were higher than they had ever been though I questioned whether the work was at the level done by other fifth grade students. As the year came to an end, Dotty made sure I would be present for a school assembly.

Why the big deal over an awards ceremony, I wondered. When the day came, Marty was called to the front of the auditorium to be presented with an award as the Most Improved Fifth Grade student at Kinsey Elementary. I was floored, and Dotty was ready to bust a few buttons over how proud she was of Marty and the progress he had shown. He remained in her classroom throughout the sixth grade.

~~~

Marty had not developed any close relationships with boys his own age. He frequently played with a boy living next door who was several years younger and seemed to look up to Marty, respecting him. At times, we found our values were at odds with the values of this family.

To broaden Marty's experience, I enrolled him in the Future Farmers of America (4-H), and soon he was working one-on-one with an older man who took a sincere interest in him. Stuart was not about to let Marty slide in his work habits and yet seemed to graciously accept his shortcomings. Every week, we would arrive on his doorstep for another lesson in woodworking or small electrical motors. In time, Marty would outgrow the lessons that Stuart offered him but this man remained an important part of our son's maturation.

Ken and I both recognized that Marty loved working outside. The small jobs we gave him helped consume some of his energy and we encouraged him to help our neighbors on days when the snow piled up in the driveways. Knowing several of the older neighbors were on limited income, I discouraged him from taking money for chores, saying I would pay him for what he accomplished. When the neighbors tried, refusing their offers became a point of pride with him. He began to see that he could bring good to other people's lives. He offered our neighbors a service they valued. He began refusing my payment for his help as well.

In time, Marty decided to take up the time-honored position delivering papers in our neighborhood. After the papers were delivered to his subscribers, he would make the rounds once a month collecting fees. One day, he stumbled off his bike and into the house.

"I got hit by a car," he moaned.

"What? You got hit by a car? Where did this happen? Are you alright? Is anything broken?

I had him sit down, crouching in front of him to check for injuries.

"I was riding my bike. This car ran into me."

"The car ran into you? Where's the driver?"

"There wasn't a driver."

"What? Was the car rolling?"

"No, mom. It was just sitting there."

"The car wasn't moving but it hit you?" Ken asked.

"Yeah, it was on the sidewalk and it hit me."

"Sooo, was the car parked?" I asked.

"Well, yeah. No one was in the car. It was sitting there."

Our adrenaline dropping, we both began to laugh.

"It sounds like you hit a parked car. Would that be correct?" Ken asked.

"You're laughing and I'm hurt. What kind of mom laughs at her injured son?" Marty demanded to know.

After bandaging how many bloody knees and hands, my relief left me laughing helplessly. Marty did not think this was funny!

It's all about perspective.

~~~

As his time in the Dotty's class came to an end, I viewed the approaching year in middle school with increasing alarm. The schedule for the students was run on a series of alarms which rang with the start and end of class. Marty would be designated as a special needs student. During each of his academic periods, he would be required to leave half way through his class for special instruction in another wing of the school. The problem was that Marty would have to be responsible for his schedule. I thought he might become so intent in watching the clock, anticipating his departure from the classroom, that he would fail to listen to what was being taught.

Children with attention deficit disorder have the ability to concentrate, excluding what is happening around them. Their attention to the television is a good example of this. The images flickering across the screen constantly change, keeping their attention. They shut out other distractions to focus on that screen. I suspected that Marty would quickly slip through the cracks in this system and we would return to his failing most subjects.

I chose to enroll him in a private school without a special education program. The teachers assured me that they could work with special needs children. As we rolled through the school year, the demands of class work often seemed beyond Marty's abilities. At times I felt my child was the only one struggling to accomplish the work, only to learn years later that three other children in that classroom struggled with learning disorders. I hoped that his struggle with school work had not damaged his confidence.

~~~

In rural Arizona, many children, both girls and boys, learn to hunt at an early age. When they are successful, the family fills their freezer with meat for the year. Ken had learned to hunt from his dad and, in turn, he now began to teach Marty.

As they drove through the woods, Marty avidly soaked up his father's instructions, learning survival and navigational skills.

Ken first took Marty quail hunting. Gambrel quail scurry across the ground, taking flight when a predator comes too close. With the years of drought and as settlement has encroached on their habitat, the population of quail has dropped. Ken and Marty returned, having walked miles for only a couple of shots.

While quail season can be done at reasonable hours of the day, pursuing a deer is best done in the early hours of the morning. As Marty turned 14, Ken thought him old enough to carry a rifle and walk much of the day. He suggested they apply for a deer tag. Rising before dawn, Marty rubbed the sleep from his eyes and stumbled into his clothing and boots.

They were particularly interested in pursuing the Coues whitetail deer found in rugged, mountainous territory. One year, they returned to the mountains of southern Arizona where Ken had hunted as a young man. Like many of the mountain ranges of southern Arizona, the slopes of the Huachuca Mountains, are deeply incised by steep ridges and rocky ravines. On the lower slopes, the terrain is not heavily forested. Groves of oak and juniper dot the grassy hillsides. Ken had learned to hunt as part of a hunting party with one man stationed below as the others climbed higher to drive the deer down toward him.

After climbing a steep ridge to a saddle below the higher ridgeline, Ken instructed Marty to find a seat overlooking the valley below. He would range across the terrain driving the deer toward his son. The Coues are known as the gray ghosts, likely to be concealed by the deep shade of an oak grove. Ken worked his way across the terrain but failed to hear a shot from Marty.

Arriving back at the saddle, he found Marty facing the ravine on the opposite side of the ridge from where Ken was driving out the deer. Without previous experience working in tandem, each had failed to understand what the other intended. Ken felt deeply disappointed for Marty when they did not return with a deer for the freezer.

On another occasion, Marty became separated from Ken and their hunting partners. He worked his way back to camp and eagerly consumed a good portion of a box of Payday candy bars before the others returned. Ken returned, chuckling over the box of empty candy wrappers and no fresh venison.

In northern Arizona, elk season with rifles rolls around each November and Marty was eager to take an elk. They chose an area with a several small lakes, well-populated with herds of elk. Throughout the morning, shots rang out as other hunters saw their opportunity. They came across a large bull elk and Marty took the shot. Ken saw the dust rise where the bullet struck the forest floor. His hands shaking, Marty shoved the rifle at Ken.

"Dad, the cartridge is jammed. I can't get it out."

Ken grabbed the rifle. He cleared the cartridge and inserted another bullet. Marty shook his head.

"Dad, I can't. You take the shot. "

Ken struck the running animal in the front quarter at a

distance of nearly 200 yards. The bull slumped to the ground. Ken cautiously approached. Seeing the animal would not rise, he waved Marty forward.

Another hunter approached. His shot had struck the animal in the leg but it was Ken's shot that had taken the bull down.

"Did you shoot this animal?" Ken asked.

"Yeah."

The hunter said nothing more. Ken looked at the massive rack. It was a beautiful animal. He wanted his son to be successful with his hunt. He remembered a time when his uncle had given him the deer they had both hit. He would help Marty find another elk.

"Take the elk," Ken said.

They did not get another shot that season. The next year they were not successful in obtaining a permit. To his great regret, Ken was never able to share that moment with Marty as he had with his father in taking his first deer.

Throughout the years, Ken emphasized to Marty that he would be satisfied with whatever Marty accomplished as long as he did his best. Marty continued to take the rifles out to the cinder pits to practice his marksmanship and this would pay off as he became an accomplished shooter.

As he passed through the middle school years, Marty made a friend. To many parents that may seem like an odd statement but up to that time, there had been no best friend other than the younger boy next door. Nate and Marty were first drawn together as the new kids among the other students. They both seemed a bit different from the other boys,

Nate quickly realized that Marty loved the outdoors and he eagerly joined in dreams of what they could accomplish if they were roaming the woods near our home.

"Mom, Nate and I have an idea. Just listen, okay?"

I kind of sensed that I wasn't going to like this idea.

"We want to go camping out by Lake Mary."

"Camping, huh?"

"Yup Just the two of us."

"I see. You don't want dad and I to come along?"

"No "

"So, why do you want to go, just the two of you, all by yourselves?"

"I guess we want to prove to you and Nate's parents that we can do this. All by ourselves. And we just want to have fun."

"Mmm," I was right. I didn't like this idea.

"We could build a campfire to keep us warm and set up a tent and fish for our dinner."

I could envision the campfire getting out of control, blazing across the countryside. Or maybe one of them getting too close to the flames.

"I don't think that this is a good idea."

Marty argued, Nate argued. I was pretty certain that Nate's parents were as unmoved as Ken and I in supporting this idea. Two years crept by, Marty gained his drive license at age seventeen. I knew that the day had to come when I would be forced to release my five-fingered grasp on the son I loved despite all his imperfections. The son who made me simultaneously laugh and want to tear my hair out in frustration. The summer after the tenth grade, we agreed to allow the boys to take their first camping trip - alone.

And somehow, they survived - without direct parental supervision. They loved their time in the woodlands of central Arizona. Marty drove an old Toyota pick-up with a camper shell while Nate drove an old Jeep. Ken worked with Marty to maintain the Toyota but the Jeep was showing its age. One day they returned with the front end barely attached to the body of the Jeep with duck tape. They laughed about how duck tape could be used for just about any problem that might arise.

There was the day, however, when Marty raced into the house, announcing, "Mom, we're going to hunt rattlesnakes. No gun this time. We're going to use a machete."

"Nope" I shook my head. "Not going to happen."

"Aww, mom!"

"Let me explain this to you. The machete is this long." I extended my arms two feet apart. "The rattlesnake can jump this far." I extended my arms another foot. "Nope! Not going to happen."

I have no idea to this day whether they hunted rattlesnakes with a machete. I wasn't invited on their camping trips but I remained adamant that they were not to hunt rattlesnakes with the long knives. Yes, we were definitely living with ADD.

The hours of living outdoors, free to follow every sane or crazy idea became a solace to Marty and Nate as they struggled with school. Nate was smart with no learning disorders but he was not motivated by the work assigned.

Marty learned to advocate for himself with his teachers, taking advantage of the special education room and the help offered. But even with the help, he barely passed his classes. I frequently spoke with the teachers on his behalf, uncertain if I was doing more harm or good in trying to help him.

In his final year, it became clear that the special education teachers would do whatever was necessary to push Marty through the doors of the school with a diploma. This included pasting together several quarters of Algebra, taken over three years, each with a barely passing grade to satisfy the math requirement for graduation. Our education system does not make allowances for functional students challenged by learning disorders when they cannot meet the standard graduation requirements.

Marty enjoyed his time in auto and wood class but again, it became apparent that with his lack of attention to detail, he would not seek a career in trades. What could he do upon graduation? We knew we had a son who was willing to work hard, who valued honesty and integrity. He knew what it meant to be the underdog, a person looked down upon, and for that reason, he reached out to others.

His older sister encouraged Marty to apply for a lifeguard position at the city pool she was managing. The night before the final exam, I quizzed him using questions from the instruction book. When he passed the test the following day, he exulted in his success. I wondered why he had not seen the value of this study technique much earlier! Regardless of tests and ADD, he became a lifeguard and seemed able to maintain a steady watch without distraction.

~~~

To this day, I wonder what possessed me when I suggested that the military might be a good option for Marty. I thought the rigors and discipline of boot camp along with chow lines and square corners on the bunks would give him a foundation for living within a structured community. Nate was already enamored with the military and Marty began to share his enthusiasm. They seemed to talk of nothing but honor and serving with pride regardless of what others thought. Their conversation went beyond a normal sense of pride to a fanaticism with all things military.

As I realized that he was serious about enlisting, the reality of the military's mission began to settle in. Once he enlisted, my son could move in a direction that might prove fatal. The military trains men to fight and to kill. In return, the men they are fighting have the same objective - to kill the soldiers on the other side. I could see Marty caught in the gunsight of an enemy soldier. Worse yet, from my love of reading history, I could see Marty at the mercy of a commander who did not value the life of every man under his command. Our discussions became heated.

"Why do you want to join the military? You might get killed!"

"Yeah, mom, I might."

"I'm not okay with that possibility!"

"Mom, what would you prefer? That I die in a head-on crash with a drunk driver or in defending my country with honor?'

"Those are my only two choices? What about choosing to live?" I asked.

No amount of arguing could change my son's mind. He was determined to enlist in the United States Marine Corps. I knew that in a few months, he would not need my consent to enlist. Finally, I made one request. He was stunned when I asked him to stay home for a year after graduation, to work and spend time with us before enlisting. He agreed. I was to savor that year, to relive the memories and dread each day that drew closer to the moment when he would board a bus for a new life.

In his last year of high school, Marty was concerned that his prescription for the drug Adderall might keep him from being allowed to enlist. He saw his use of Adderall as a weakness even though he recognized that the drug improved his focus on the tasks assigned. He asked to discontinue using the drug. Rather than making the decision, I asked him to discuss this with his doctor. After discussing the purpose of the drug and his future plans, the doctor suggested that he would agree to this on one condition. If Marty's grades began to fall and he was not completing the class work, I was to report back to the doctor. The doctor would take the responsibility for placing Marty back on Adderall. I sat back, marveling at the doctor's intuition. He understood that I was tired of being on the front line in keep Marty on track. He knew Marty would respect him and work hard to keep this agreement. Yet, the agreement allowed Marty a back way out if he was unable to keep up in his assignments. They shook hands on the agreement. Marty finished the year with passing grades.

He spend the last year at home, working as a lifeguard, helping his dad around the house and hanging out with friends. As part of his duties, he agreed to lifeguard for a group of older women who practiced their aquatic exercise early in the morning. He would stumble out of bed before dawn and climb on his bike, riding five miles across town to open the pool, slowly waking while the ladies kicked and paddled.

One morning, riding through the dim glow half asleep, he failed to see the post of a stop sign in his path. He slowly regained consciousness laying on the sidewalk and realized that the stop sign had somehow moved into his path. Or at least that was his version of the accident.

He opened the pool, his face and shirt covered with blood. I'm not certain he was seeing straight but he climbed into the chair without bothering to remove all traces of blood. The ladies were horrified that their strong, young lifeguard had been injured! They clucked over him in their concern as he maintained the strong, tough image he had once sported through the halls of the high school, almost daring anyone to cross his path.

He later returned to the stop sign, proud to find that the post no longer stood at a ninety degree angle from the sidewalk. I can only imagine the force it took to bend the metal post

This was the son I sent off to join the United States Marine Corps. In raising him, I laughed and cried. I learned about love and faith, believing God had created a young man with promise who would undoubtedly not become what I intended. I could not believe those years had come to an end.

A Man Off to War

2002

What do you say to a son who calls home, asking you to pray that he will pass the final exam in his effort to graduate from training camp? He tells you a failing grade would cause the Marine Corps to discharge him. He could be sent home, never having to face combat. Most mothers would say this sounded good. Yet, this is important to your son, his chance to prove himself for the first time, after having stepped from the protection and love of his family.

I stared out into the darkness. "Father, you know how much I love Marty. I really don't want to see him placed in harm's way but I know how much this means to him. Father, I don't know what to ask? You know what is best here. Help me to trust you for the best and help my son to do well on his test.

The next evening Marty called.

"Mom, you're not going to believe what happened!
"Yeah?"

"Someone broke into the computer system, you know, hacked it? They wiped out all the grades. The commander says we all pass since they can't do anything about the break-in! I passed, mom!"

"Wow."

My excitement for my son was underwhelming! "Father, I hope you know what you're doing here!" I thought.

Marty loved boot camp. The training was harsh. He recited stories of sleepless nights, crows eating their food supplies. Struggling to swim while weighed down with a pack. All of it pushed his physical endurance and, unlike his academic struggle, this was a challenge where he excelled!

He moved on to advanced training in combat and weapons handling. There would be no vocational training for this man, he was to be a grunt, an infantryman. He was trained to fight.

One morning, he led a team of soldiers into a building. After blowing the door with a flash grenade, they moved down a hall. As the hallway split in two directions, he waved two men toward one end while he and a partner scurried the opposite direction. Entering the room, his weapon jammed and he sank to one knee to clear it even as he yelled at his partner to cover him. A moment later he raised his eyes into the dark bore hole of a pistol barrel twelve inches from his face. Behind the grip were the smiling eyes of the trainer as he pulled the trigger.

Marty wore a large goose egg on his forehead from the rubber bullet for a week as a reminder that one always checks to see if he is covered before becoming distracted by a jammed firearm.

When the time came to be assigned to a company of

Marines, Marty and several other men stepped forward to be met by three officers, firing questions about their training and goals as a Marine. Marty answered the questions crisply with a confidant manner. His lieutenant noted that this was a Marine's Marine. He chose Marty to join Alpha Company, 1st Battalion, 5th Marines. The battalion was assigned to Kuwait in anticipation of the invasion of Iraq.

2003
A Time For War and a Time For Peace

Marty called when he could, after waiting in line for an hour in the sand of Kuwait. As February, 2003 passed, the men of the United States Marines and the US Army massed along the border with Iraq, waiting for the signal to surge north toward Bagdad. Saddam dickered with the United Nations over whether he was complying with their demands to hand over his supply of lethal weapons of mass destruction.

The calendar turned to the month of March. In our mountain town, the outdoor temperature began to rise, steadily warming. In Arizona, we know hot weather. I may live at 7,000 feet elevation but driving south into the deserts of southern Arizona, the temperature can rise to 120 degrees in the summer, very much like the deserts of Iraq.

As the temperatures began to rise in Iraq, I feared for our men as they waited for the United Nations to make their final resolutions regarding Saddam and Iraq. Marty did his best to reassure me that he was drinking gallon after gallon of water. Yet, I knew the weight he would carry when they moved across the border and the moisture that would leak from his body, leading to dehydration.

Was it futile to hope that Saddam would stand down and comply with the demands? Again, I questioned how to pray. Ultimately, we pray for peace even as we know that there is only One who can bring real peace when we surrender our will to him. I struggled to surrender.

"Father, please take care of him! Keep those bullets away from him!" Even with my mindless requests, a quiet voice echoed through my mind.

"Ruth, what of the mothers of the soldiers on the other side? What are they praying for their sons?"

War is as much a conflict for those who love as well as those who fight.

On March 20, 2003 our men surged across the border. Like every other military mother, my emotions twisted in turmoil over the thought of my son, riding in the back of a bumpy, fume-filled metal box as they crossed the sands of Kuwait into Iraq.

Within days, the Marines had advanced to the outskirts of Sadr City, only to be held back while the Army negotiated tough terrain on the western approach to Bagdad. When the 1st Battlion, 5th Marines finally entered Bagdad, they stumbled into an ambush, trapped in a narrow street, bullets and rocket-propelled grenades raining down on them. But even here, God had heard the prayers of mothers for their sons. God sent his angels into that combat zone to protect the young men as they returned the bullets and rocket-propelled grenades raining down on them. With God's intervention, they eventually found refuge in one of Saddam's palaces.*

Days later, Marty called me to report that he had taken his first bath in weeks in the lake outside the palace. He was sure that nothing had ever felt quite so good as he washed two weeks of grime from his body. As days of combat turned into days of guard duty, the rumors began to circulate that 1/5 would return home earlier than expected.

During his last year at home, before his enlistment, Marty had been dating a young lady. They had talked of marriage. We traded phone calls when Marty called, each of us hoping for his safe return. At the same time, our eldest daughter's husband had been deployed to southern Arizona, releasing men to combat overseas. Our family was learning the rhythms of war in phone calls and the quiet of missing the one you love.

The son that came home was different from the son Ken put on the bus, riding off to boot camp. Marty carried himself differently. Body posture, stride and the short haircut said, 'This is a Marine!'

Today, we laugh as we see a young man swaggering through a crowded room. Their demeanor shouts, 'Marine!'

But there was another side to Marty. He talked of the friends he had made in the 1/5. Young men who easily allowed him into their company, inviting him to bonfires on

---

* Lt. Carey Cash, US Navy Chaplain, has written an excellent account of the Alpha 1/5 Marine Battalion in their invasion of Iraq and God's providence in this ambush. We highly recommend his book, A Table in the Presence.

the beach with girls and alcohol flowing freely. Our son like to drink beer. This was not something we encouraged in our house even though one of us might have a glass of wine now and then.

"Mom, the Lieutenant had a talk with me. He thinks I've got leadership potential. But he said my friends are real losers. One of them got busted down in rank in a court marshal. The Lieutenant wants me to hang out with the other squad leaders but they treat me like crap. They watch porn and drink in the evenings. I don't want to be around them. The guy who got busted may never be much but he treats me with respect."

I listened, thinking about what he valued in people. I was proud of him for looking at a person's character rather than their rank.

At home, he hung out with his best friend and his fiancé. He visited his mentor, a Sergeant Major in the Marine Reserve. But every night he came home to sleep in his bed and hang out with us. I wondered if life seemed a little too slow at home compared to rattling through Iraq in the back of a humvee, always ready for a sudden attack. If he had post traumatic stress syndrome, we did not see the standard markers of nightmares, difficulty sleeping, loss of composure, anger and flashbacks.

Ken and Marty spent time talking about faith and his responsibility to God. One afternoon, Ken explained that how he treated the freedom to drink, to smoke, to behave without restraints was an indication of one's relationship with God. We noticed that after their conversation, Marty didn't touch another beer, leaving four bottles out of a six pack sitting in his closet.

One day, I came into the livingroom to find Marty sitting on the floor quietly talking to our cocker spaniel as he stroked her head. I stopped abruptly. This was a dog who had feared Marty, avoiding him due to his rough treatment of her. Yet, now she seemed to accept his attention as he gently stroked her head. In that moment, I recognized my son was growing up. He was learning he did not have to show aggression to prove how tough he could be as a man.

I was reminded of a verse from Zechariah, the first verse Marty memorized. 'Not by might, nor by strength but by my spirit, says the Lord.'

Before he had entered the Marines, he had lived the tough image, seeking might, power and dominance. Watching him with the dog, I thought that he might be learning the real essence of strength.

The night he left, the kid next door held a party with alcohol, music and lots of people flowing in and out of his house. We were sitting in our front room, quietly talking until the time came to take Marty to the bus station to catch a ride back to Camp Pendleton. The door opened and in walked two young men we had never seen before. They stopped in the middle of the livingroom, looked around, shrugged and muttered, 'wrong house.' They turned and left.

Before I could rise from the couch, Marty was next door, jerking the neighbor kid into the street. Porch lights began to pop on as he loudly berated the kid using a string of profanity. I stood at the door, my mouth open in amazement at how quickly my son had moved. The realization of the profanity slowly settled in.

"Marty, watch your mouth!" I called. "No cussing!"

I sounded like a crotchety old lady, waving my cane at a young kid. This was my son. How dare he talk like that? The profanity flowing from his mouth was a reflection of the environment that he had lived in for six months. Again, I felt slow to understand that my son was no longer a little boy, under my instruction. He was a man who would take care of his parents. The kid next door had no doubt where he stood and what would happen if such an incident occurred again.

After Marty returned to Camp Pendleton, we began to hear stories about the beach parties and two or three young ladies. There was Amber 1 and Amber 2, there was Christina. The girls were working hard to separate him from his fiancé. They swore that Marty treated them better than the young men they had known growing up - the same young men in Marty's squad. In telling us this, he laughed and said that they like how he opened the door for them and treated them with respect.

2004

Six months of long days and training at Camp Pendleton rolled by and deployment loomed again. The battles in Iraq were not going as well as the initial invasion. Marty's unit was assigned to Fallujah, a spiritual center for Islam in Iraq. I believed the battle was more than bullets and guns. This would be a battle of spiritual forces as well. A battle that demanded prayer. The military, as an institution, does not know prayer, they only know force and firepower.

Within days of entering Fallujah, an incident occurred that would light a match, setting off a battle that would disintegrate into squads of men hunting each other in deserted streets and homes.

An embedded reporter later told me that an officer had paused to watch a young woman walk to the river. He was simply curious as to her route but Iraqi young men who lingered nearby watching him believed otherwise. He did not know that she intended to bath in the river. Angrily, the crowd of men approached a commander and shouted their displeasure. Shots were fired. A melee ensued and the hostility grew until the city was engulfed in full-scale conflict. Families fled their homes and squads of men exchanged gunfire with the militants around a key mosque in town.

Most likely you won't read about that exchange in the news media. Only those on the ground saw the incident quickly grow beyond control. Our soldiers began barricading themselves in houses, using whatever they could find to strengthen their positions, furniture, bags of rice, cement blocks. Some days, the men did not get more than one meal a day, some days nothing as the fighting was too fierce.

In the evening, an officer would assemble his men into a squad, creeping through the streets and empty houses to wait in ambush. The militants were doing the same. On patrols through the streets, our men understood that any Iraqi could carry an improvised explosive device. If a man refused to back down when given an order, he was shot for fear he would set off an explosion, sending shrapnel into the soldiers. At times, it was simply too dangerous for the bodies to be retrieved and the next day the patrols would be forced to check each corpse to ensure that the body in turn was not used to hide explosives that could be detonated by remote control.

Our son was one of those men, walking the streets, creeping through the buildings in ambush. He dreaded the moments when he had to check a corpse. He told us about the days of deprivation and fear held at bay when he returned home again after a six month deployment.

I ached for him as I watched for signs of PTSD. As with the previous visit, he seemed to settle into the routine, to sleep, to interact without flashbacks to that terrible field of battle.

Not too long after he got home, I confronted him about his first tour.

"So, tell me about your invasion of Bagdad again."

"Oh, mom! No big deal. I told you about how we went in and .."

"Yeah, I remember that. Now, tell me about the ambush you were caught in."

"What ambush?"

"The one where your unit was caught in a narrow street under heavy fire."

"Aww, no, that wasn't me. Yeah, there were some soldiers who had a rough time but I just sat at an intersection that day."

Raising one eyebrow, I pulled a book from behind my

back and shook it at him.

"I don't think so. I've read 1/5 Alpha was caught in an ambush, narrow street, bullets, RPGs! You want to revise your story?"

"Oh!" He looked a little sheepish. "You weren't supposed to find out about that one. How did you know about that?"

"This book." I flipped it around so that he could see the cover. "Do you know a Lieutenant Carey Cash?'

"Carey? You're talking about Lieutenant Cash? Oh, man, he is really cool, mom!"

I had obviously hit the sweet spot. The words spilled out of Marty as he enthusiastically sang the praises of a chaplain the men loved. This chaplain taught from God's word and brought compassion to the men caught in the grip of evil, fighting for their lives. He lived with them, listened to them and spoke to them in a way they could understand.

Carey spilled the truth of what had happened in the Kuwait desert across the American landscape with his book, In The Presence of the Enemy. In Kuwait, as they waited for the command to cross the border, their Bible studies started with just a handful of men, including Marty. As the weeks passed, the tension building, the number of men in the Bible studies grew to hundreds, many choosing to confess their sins, asking to be baptized. Carey told how he had ridden with the men of the 1/5 as they fought their way north toward Bagdad and into one of Saddam's palaces. Carey was a unique chaplain, preaching the truth rather than a passive message of good feelings without a solid foundation. Word of mouth would cause book sales to multiply as people across the country read of the amazing work of God to the men of 1/5 Alpha and his deliverance in the face of a deadly ambush.

After that day, our son began to confide in us about what had happened in Fallujah, seeming confident that I would not react badly to the grim stories he told. One day, he seemed a bit embarrassed.

"Mom, I need to tell you something. Now, it's no big deal but I guess my commander made a big deal out of it. I don't want you to go blabbing your mouth off about it! It was no big deal, you understand?"

"Huh, you want to give me a clue as to what you're talking about?"

"I guess I'm getting a medal."

"Okay. And this is a big deal?"

"I was just looking out for some guys. They said I did something brave."

I kept asking questions till we had the whole story. Alpha company was patrolling the Fallujah 500, a stretch of open ground that left them exposed. Somehow, several men at the back of the column had gotten separated from the rest of the platoon. Shots rang out. Several militants were standing behind a wall, elevated above the street level, shooting down at our men. Our Marines were pinned down, unable to move. The two officers looked back and one asked, "What do we want to do here? Think they can fight their way out?"

Marty didn't wait for the answer. Grabbing his 50 caliber semi-automatic weapon along with a belt of cartridges, he ran back toward the men under fire. As he ran, the militants began to shoot at him, the bullets kicking up the dust around his feet. He swerved one way, back another until he reached a slight rise in the open ground. Throwing himself to the ground, he set the weapon on its stand and began to return fire.

The citation says that due to his accurate fire, he eliminated several of the combatants, lifting the ambush off the men trapped in the cross-fire. The citation is the Naval Commendation for Valor Under Combat.

Looking at my son, I demanded, "How could you be so stupid? You could have been killed!"

"Mom, one of my buddies was trapped back there. I decided that he wasn't going to die that day."

I got it. I told my son how very proud I was of him, though he was scaring the wits out of me with the risks he took. This was not the first time he had taken a risk, exposing himself to enemy fire.

He understood that his death would take him in the presence of God. He knew that many of the men he fought with did not have that assurance. Some of the Marines in his unit had wives and children while he remained single. As he explained, Marines don't think about how they are fighting for freedom or any such ideal as the bullets are flying around them. They fight for the Marine on their left and the Marine on their right. Marty was prepared to give his life for another man.

2005

Returning from Fallujah, Marty had served two deployments. He shouldn't have to return, right? Ken and I kept telling our friends that this was military tradition, even as we failed to understand that the world we had grown up in had changed.

On his last visit home, Ken and Marty once again spent an hour many mornings sitting on the back porch talking about life and faith.

"Marty, I've shared God's Word with you. Now, it's your turn. What can you share with me?

Marty thought for a moment. "There is a verse I've been working on. It says that we should not fear the one who can kill our bodies. We should fear the one who can take our souls. Dad, I think that means that I shouldn't worry about getting killed. I should work on my relationship with God. He is the one who holds the ultimate control over my soul."*

Ken was thrilled to think that his son was reading God's word and applying what he read to his life. He mentioned to Marty that the women in the Tuesday morning Bible study had been faithfully praying for him as had many friends across the country.

That Tuesday, Marty sauntered into the kitchen at church and quietly listened as the Bible study teacher prayed to end the meeting. As the women raised their heads, he stepped into the room and spoke to them.

* Matthew 10:28

"I'm Marty Mortenson, the son of Ruth and Ken Mortenson."

A couple of women laughed and one said, "We know. We've watched you grow up." He grinned at them.

"I understand you've been praying for me. I just wanted to say I really appreciate that. Thank you. We need it over there."

He turned to leave and they called him back to pray for him as he stood there, his shoulders and face rigid in determination. Later, several women told us they just want to hug him but thought maybe Marty would be one embarrassed Marine if a bunch of women started hugging him!

Once again, he was called to deploy to Ramadi, Iraq. We were stunned. As they climbed off the plane after their deployment in Fallujah, a reporter from National Public Radio stuck her microphone in Marty's face and asked, "Do you want to go back?"

"No!" He strode away without another word. Now, as he faced a third deployment to Iraq, we talked about how he felt. With resignation, he said he had a job to do and no choice but to do it. Friends took one last photo of him as he shouldered his pack to join the line of Marines boarding the flight for Iraq. His smile in that photo is wistful and sad.

We later learned that he told his sister that with this deployment he did not think he would be coming back alive.

Arguing with God, Losing

Bagdad, the city of a thousand tales. Fallujah, a city destroyed by violence. And then, Ramadi. The names associated with each deployment rolled off our lips. They were the places that Marty was stationed. Beyond that we knew little other than what we heard on the evening news and read in the newspaper.

For their third deployment, 1/5 Alpha was assigned to Ramadi. I groaned, knowing that the assignment was in the vaunted triangle of death, a region associated with the Sunni Muslims. The region had remained violent after the initial invasion by U.S. forces. Once again 1/5 Alpha was assigned to confront men who hated the United States and wished only to kill our soldiers. The 1/5 was sent to Ramadi to put down the insurgency and win the hearts of the population.

A week after he left Flagstaff for his third deployment, I was once again seized by fear for Marty's safety. I could not escape the thought that he might not survive. If I mentioned this to Ken, my husband told me I was not trusting God for Marty's safety. People across the country were praying for Marty by name. He reminded me that the Bible says to ask what we will and God will answer according to his will.

Ken was praying that God would be honored. He asked that God would be glorified through whatever happened with Marty. The nagging thought that God might choose to act through Marty's death crept into his mind. He set that aside, choosing to believe in faith that Marty would come through unscathed.

Desperately, I cried out to God to save my son. In return, I sensed God asking whether I could trust him? I argued my love for my son and the crushing grief if God should choose to take him.

Again, a quiet voice, the voice I've heard since I was a small child asked, "Will you trust me?"

Could I trust God to love Marty more than I did? Could I accept that God might have plans other than returning my son safely to us?

"No! No! NO!" I argued. "Don't take my boy! God, I need him. I can not bear to lose him. I can not bear the thought, I could not bear the grief!"

Again, God asked, "Do you trust me?"

"Oh, God not this! Don't ask me to do this."

But what could I do about it? If God chose to take my son, I could not stop him. I could not fly over to Bagdad and stand in front of my son, warning the Iraqis to keep their bullets and bombs away from him. I had to trust God. Every parent faces this fear from the time their children are born. Ultimately, if we are honest with ourselves, we know we cannot stop God if he chooses to take our child. But I prayed once again.

"Father, I love this boy. It would break my heart if you took him."

"Who loves him more, you or me?"

The visual image of Jesus hanging from the cross in my place stood before me. God had given his son, the most perfect being, to take my place in receiving the punishment for sin. He took on himself the sins of my son, dying in Marty's place as penance for his sin. This could be said for every man and woman who comes to the foot of the cross and seeks God's forgiveness.

"Who loves him more?"

"That is unfair," I raged. "You know there is only one answer to that. How can I say anything than that you love him more."

"Then, can you trust me to know what is best for your son?"

"Oh, Lord Jesus, I know I must place him in your hands but losing him will break my heart. What choice do I have?"

After pleading with God for days, I felt as if God had taken me through a wringer. A peace of sorts came to stay even as I dreaded the thought that Marty might not survive. I accepted the fact that this was in God's hands and there was nothing I could do but choose to trust him.

I sat talking with one of our employees one day in the shop. His wife was facing the same struggle as her son served in the Marine Corps.

"I choose to trust God," I told Wayne. "What choice do I have?"

"You won't handle this so calmly if something happens

to Marty," he objected. "I bet you'll have a much more difficult time than you think."

Stunned, I sat looking at him. His comments forced me to realize that we were under observation from those around us. Could I handle such a difficult loss, knowing so many were watching? I once again asked God to guard my heart and mind if he called me to stand in the sight of our community without giving way to hysteria and to grief.

On April 19, Marty and his fellow Marines were sent out on patrol through the streets of Ramadi. Suddenly, an I.E.D. exploded. Patrick, one of the Marines, fell to the ground in agony, grasping his bloodied boot and leg. Two of his comrades restrained the injured man as Marty and another Marine began to cut away the boot to inspect the damage. The wounded man screamed that they were hurting him, alternating with cussing at the insurgents that had planted the bomb and indicating what he thought of them with a single raised digit. One of the Marines grabbed Patrick's arm as he tried to push Marty away, screaming, "They're trying to help you, man. Shut up."

Later, after the wounded man had been evacuated, the men relived the incident, laughing at how the Marine was determined to vent his defiance toward his attackers, knowing witnesses would report the details to those who disguised the explosive.

On April 20, 2005, a report reached the commanders in Ramadi that a group of al-Queda members were meeting at a local café to make plans. A cache of weapons was stored at the site as well. The report called for a quick strike force to convoy quickly through the streets of Ramadi to capture whatever they could find at the site.

Marty chose to be the last to climb aboard the troop carrier. This was his outlook on life: He put himself in a dangerous position to protect the lives of those with him. He thought he could give others a chance to live and return to their families if he was taken.

The standard approach to such a patrol is to send three streams of vehicles, one by the direct route. Two other lines of troop convoys pace the lead column through the streets on either side, hoping to confuse the insurgents about where to lay ambushes or improvised explosive devices. The transport rolled out of the compound into the streets of Ramadi.

At the rear of the vehicle, Marty was ready to jump to the ground as the troops charged into the café. One of the men in the company dropped a cigarette as the transport roared down the street. Marty bent to pick it up, handing it back to the other man. As the second vehicle, containing Marty and his fellow Marines, passed a critical point, an explosion crescendoed off the buildings surrounding the compound.

Turning to look back, Eric, one of his friends, remembers thinking, "That had better not be Marty."

In the transport, Josh, the Marine next to Marty began to regain a sense of where he sat after the shock of the percussion wave had passed. Glancing around, he noticed Marty slumped over, blood streaming from his head. Jumping to the ground, he threw Marty over one shoulder and began to stumble from the scene of the explosion as others tended to Matt Canon, a second wounded man. Once Josh reached a safe location, he laid Marty carefully on the ground. A medic rushed up as Josh struggled to keep Marty's airway open. Within minutes, the medic had called an air transport to the scene and Marty was flown to a field hospital in Bagdad where the doctors struggled to save his life.

In the explosion, a piece of shrapnel had penetrated the side of Marty's head, entering just under his helmet. He lived for several hours, before succumbing to his wounds.

In the hours that followed, the men of 1/5 Alpha felt the impact of losing two men. Along with Marty, Matt had been killed by the attack. Another Marine sustained a shrapnel wound to his leg. Marty had sheltered the man next to him from further injury even though this Marine was well over six feet tall. Marty and Matt had taken the shrapnel that would have pierced the other Marines as Marty bent down to retrieve the cigarette. In the days that followed, each of the men in that transport would be asking themselves many questions about their own fortune in surviving while two of their comrades were gone. Most struggled with a sense of survivor's guilt.

Later that afternoon, I arrived home from work and was sitting at my computer. My husband came in the back door around 5:00, at least an hour earlier than his usual arrival. I jumped up to greet him, pleasantly surprised that he was home early.

"What?" he asked. "You want me to leave and come back in a hour?"

Laughing, I grabbed his hand and led him into the front room. We began to talk about the day and the clients we had encountered at work. Ken was facing this window when he muttered, "uh, oh."

I jumped up to see what might be happening out on the street that caused him to look so startled.

Two Marines were crossing the porch toward our front door. In that moment, you know. The Marines do not send their officers to your home to tell you your son is gravely injured. As you go to the front door, you know what is coming.

For many, death is so unexpected. Oh, we knew the risk of Marty going into a war zone. We knew he could die. Even so, death is a shock. So final.

That moment of comfortable conversation disintegrated. I ran to the front door and flung it open.

"Is this what I think this is," I demanded to know as the Marines approached. They looked a bit startled.

"Ma'am, is this the home of Mrs. Ruth Mortenson?"

"Yes! Are you here for the reason I think you are here?"

"Ma'am, are you Mrs. Ruth Mortenson?"

"Look, just tell me what you have to say," I demanded.

"Ma'am, are you Mrs. Ruth Mortenson?"

"Yes!" Wasn't that obvious?

They asked if they could come in and we all stepped inside.

In that moment, I mentally reached out with both my hands, silently speaking to God.

"Father, do not let me go! You have brought us to this place. I am reaching out to grab the hem of your garment.* Please, don't loosen your grasp on me. Don't let me go!"

After they closed the door, I said, "Gentlemen, I am a Christian. My faith is in God and he will give me the strength to hear anything you have to say to me."

The Marines began their official announcement.

"Ma'am, we regret to inform you that at fifteen hundred, there was an incident in the town of Ramadi..."

The official language of a military death is so structured. The men could not simply says my son had been killed. I had to curb my impatience as they fulfilled their duty.

I walked over and sat on the couch as the chaplain sat down opposite me. I looked up to see tears welling up in his eyes and he struggled to speak. We learned he had just returned from Iraq and had been assigned to this duty. I reached out to lay a hand on his arm.

"I am so sorry that you have to do this. I cannot imagine how difficult this must be as you carry the memories of all you have experienced over there in the last few months."

He nodded and wiped his eyes.

---

* Mark 5:27-30

A Question

This is our story of raising, loving and losing our son. Every parent who has lost a child has their own story.

Take a moment and ask that question of yourself as many people have asked us. How does a parent survive the loss of a child they have loved and nurtured? How would you react to the loss of your child, to the loss of someone you love deeply?

As a Christian, I turn to the Bible and the scriptures I believe to be God's word to us. In those pages, I find the story of a man who was asked not only to give up his son but to be the instrument of his death. Such a request would seem inhumane. Through years of study, I knew the answer to surviving the death of my child lay within the pages of the Bible.

Before I tell you what I learned through Marty's death, I would like to tell you the story of Abraham. I believe his story holds the key to understanding God's purpose in our loss.

Come! Step with me into the land of Canaan hundreds of years before the birth of Jesus Christ and what some would call the common era.

Part II

Abraham: A Journey
Genesis 22:1-3

One foot at a time, planted in the grit. Fine grains drifted upward, across his feet with each step. He grimaced against the discomfort of the sharp rock that wedged between the leather strap and his foot. Trudging forward, the heat of the sun rose from the sandy plain, first warming, then baking his aging skin.

He squinted against the sun's glare, seeking shade where the men and his son might turn aside and rest a few minutes. The servants could trudge over the heat-baked plain throughout the morning. He was not overly concerned for them. They were men and as servants subject to his plans. His son, a young man still, needed the respite that a bit of shade would offer.

He pried the rock from his sandal with a bony finger. His feet had paced this land for a hundred years, turning his soles into leather, worthy of an animal's hide. Still, there was no need to allow the pebble to grind against the skin till it wore a sore spot that would cause him to limp.

Overhead, a raucous cry caught the attention of the

old man. He gazed upward, watching the flight of the hawk as the bird drifted along the wind currents, searching for prey. He thought back to times when he had felt like the prey of powerful men, of times when he searched for refuge and found little shelter in a lie. Sarah had shared those days, knowing his fear and confusion.

Sarah remained back in the camp, ignorant of God's command and of Abraham's intentions. She had supervised the assembly of supplies for this journey, instructing the servants as they packed provisions for the miles ahead.

"How many days will you be gone?" she asked him again.

"Seven days, I think." He gazed into the distance, refusing to meet her eyes. "Here," she called to a young servant. "More raisins in that pouch."

She turned to another, observing the force he poured into the wood he was splitting.

"Don't you think you will find firewood in the mountains? Leave us this wood and spare the young men."

"Sarah, leave it," he said gently. "I will take the wood."

She studied his face. He raised his hand to gently push back a strand of dry, gray hair that fluttered across her forehead, catching on her eyelashes. Her brown eyes solemnly sought the secret he hid deep within his mind.

"There is something about you," she said. "What are you doing? What are you about, Abraham?"

He looked away, silent.

"Abraham!" She spoke sharply. "We have never kept anything from each other. What is it? What troubles you?"

"Nothing," he said. "God will provide."

She studied him again.

"What are you seeking?" she asked. "Why this journey?"

He failed to reply as Isaac raced around the corner of a tent toward his parents.

"I've filled my water skins," he called. "These skins are tightly sealed. See, nothing leaks from them."

Sarah smiled at her son as she cupped his head, drawing him near.

"You!" She laughed at his eager face. "You are getting so tall. I can hardly believe you're old enough to make this journey with your father." She turned to Abraham. "Take care of him."

Sarah turned quickly and hurried toward two servant girls grinding wheat into flour.

"How much do you have now?" Her voice cracked with emotion as she bent over them.

Abraham gazed at her bent back. How could he make this journey that God required? How could he take Isaac from her? If she knew what was required she would bind her son to her, refusing to let him leave her side.

Sarah was everything he required in a wife. She had complied with his demands when he faced down powerful men. She had agreed to lie to the Pharoah's officials in Egypt, saying she was his sister. Their relationship was close but she was no sister. Companion, lover and wife, the one who walked every step of life's journey with him. He was about to betray her trust.

The men bound the firewood to the back of a donkey.

Sacks of food were strapped to another animal, water on two more. He hoped they would find the springs at Hebron running full. He hoped for every delay in finding the springs.

His wife had grown silent, watching the preparations. Her eyes followed his movements in checking the packs even as his men had already checked them, twice. He straightened up and stared at her across the animal's back.

"Sarah," he breathed.

She waited but he bent back to his task. He seemed unable to say more than her name. She shook her head at his silence. He motioned to the two young men with him to grasp the bridles of their pack animals, pulling them forward. Once more, he stopped. He turned to look at her.

Abraham moved forward. Isaac ran to his mother.

"Mama, I will see you in seven days, maybe six. I will see you! Don't worry!"

Tears streamed down Sarah's face as she clutched his arm.

"My son!"

"Mama!" Isaac tore his arm from her grasp, laughing. He followed the animals, turning once to look back at her, waving eagerly. She watched till they were out of sight.

The Covenant

His eyes stared into the darkness, his body aching from the cold ground. The night seemed to stretch longer than the hours of darkness he had endured, wrapped in sheep skins against the cool night air. He searched the darkness of the eastern sky for some faint change in the deep hues of early morning, indicating that dawn would finally come.

The pack animals stirred against their restraints, cropping the sparse grass that pushed through the desert floor. In an hour, they would move out, pushing north toward Hebron. The men still slept, worn from the hours of travel the previous day. He was in no hurry to wake them. Abraham did not welcome the journey's end.

His eyes strayed toward the mound that was Isaac, buried in his own sheep skin. With each breath, a slight shushing crept from his son toward Abraham's ear. In, out, the boy's lungs rose with the breath of life signaling that he still lived. Abraham would sleep no more this night. The years had stripped him of unbroken sleep. His aching body urged him to frequently change positions. Or his bladder urged him to rise and void the ache into the sand. His thoughts, especially on this journey troubled him, chasing sleep from a disturbed mind.

His son, the one most precious, would have a few more minutes to sleep as he thought of the day when Isaac's arrival had been announced. He shifted slightly to ease his bladder and the pain in his shoulders.

Genesis 15:1-19

The day Isaac's birth had been announced had been like any day with the men following the herds of sheep and goats. The women had worked around the camp. Abram had been more restless than usual that day, moving through the tents, discontent with the daily routine. He was troubled as if something, maybe someone, remained at the edge of sight, not quite visible. Yet, he sensed their presence.

Settling into the rugs that made his bed, Abram had fallen into a deep sleep, crying out as his dream moved him. When he woke, he moved quickly toward the herds of sheep and goats, selecting two animals. He called for his men to bring a heifer along with a dove and pigeon. Settling around the campfire, the men watched as Abram pulled out a long sharp knife, drawing it against the mighty arteries hidden in the corded necks of each animal. As the blood stained the dust around them, Abram struggled to slice each animal in half, leaving only the two birds whole. He laid the halves of each animal side by side. Throughout that afternoon, he sat with the carcasses spread around him, driving off the vultures that were drawn by the smell of blood. Flicking his hands at the flies that clustered over the decaying carcasses, he waited as dusk settled over the campsite.

The rays of the setting sun crept up the rock out croppings that littered the brown plain. The uppermost branches of the large trees seemed to seize the last shred of light, before releasing it to the dim glow that muted the hills surrounding the camp. And then, that dim glow was snuffed out, leaving the night pitch black, lit only by a large campfire at the edge of the tents.

Dust, mixed with acrid smoke, swirled through the encampment, holding the tents in a black haze. Mothers hushed the voices of their children at play. Hunting dogs crept beneath the loose folds of tent, their eyes all that shone in the reflection of a red glare from the fire.

And then, before the startled eyes of his family and his servants, a dim glow shone out of the darkness as if an obscure form, carrying a pot of coals, appeared to move through the stinking meat and clotted blood. A wisp of smoke passed over one carcass. A flame shot up from the pot of coals, illuminating the camp and prostate forms near the tents. The darkness seemed to hold a physical presence and Abram groaned as if in pain and misery. Those of the encampment froze in place, afraid to move, afraid that the physical weight of this unseen Presence would overwhelm them, driving them into the dust. For hours they hugged the ground in fear, in obeisance to the Presence until Abram rose from his position near the glowing coals of the campfire to summon them closer.

Abram stared at the sky above, directing their attention to the myriad of stars that swept across the expanse. God had spoken to Abram, promising his descendants would be as numerous as the stars overhead. His descendants would inherit the land he now roamed, seeking water and pasture for his flocks.

Abram knew he had no heir other than an elder in Damascus who would receive his estate. But God had promised that his descendants would inherit this land and to inherit there must be a son. Abram staked his obedience to this promise.

Sarai
Genesis 16:1-6

As time passed, the older servants shook their heads, watching Sarai move slowly through the encampment. Abram's wife was no longer of child bearing age. Her gray hair reflected the setting sun, indicating the long years she had followed this man, Abram.

Sarai had struggled to believe. An unseen Spirit had spoken to her husband, pulling him from Ur, leading him out into the desert. She had struggled to share Abram's vision as his servants packed the donkeys with provisions. He had turned seventy-five years old when he contemplated the move into the desert.

The life of her family, of the marketplace, of the narrow streets was all she knew. Her family kept herds of sheep and goats as their livelihood but she had never followed the herds as did the nomads that drifted past the walls of Ur. She slept in the same bed, beneath the same shadows every night.

She turned to look back at her family as Abram's caravan stalked steadily toward the horizon. She had raised one hand in farewell. Her sister had raised a hand in return.

Nothing more. No one crying in protest as she was swept away from all she knew in her younger years. She knew she would not see them again as she turned to follow Abram.

As a girl, Sarai had seen Abram in the market as she haggled for her family's food. He had been driving several sheep toward the butcher, intending to seek a good price. He had smiled as he passed her, aware of her admiration. He seemed to straighten a little without intending to preen before the beautiful young woman.

She was not unaware that young men watched her each day as she moved through the market, making her purchases. Some smiled timidly while others competed to show their brawn in handling heavy loads. Some pretended to ignore her even as they were aware of her every movement in their presence.

As she moved toward home, Abram stepped into her path, blocking the route through the stalls of vendors haggling with their customers. He smiled down at her. She sensed that he would treat her with more respect than some of her friends received under the heavy hand of their husbands. A woman's place could be difficult but Abram's smile bore a gentle respect even as his lean body spoke of a life lived in the open.

Within two weeks, he had spoken to her father. The haggling over the bride price had been short. Abram seemed content to pay nearly what her father had asked. For many of her friends, the negotiations had consumed weeks. By the time a marriage had taken place, her friends had felt as if they were nothing more than one of their family's livestock.

Sarai smiled faintly. Her bride price did not mean that her husband was deficient in driving a bargain. The merchants of Ur, and then Haran, had quickly learned that he was a man to be respected for his care of the livestock as well as in their negotiations with him.

They had grown in the first years of marriage, learning each other's ways. But she had been as amazed as any of their friends when Abram announced that they would be leaving Ur. Only his nephew, Lot, had seemed to be interested in following them into the wilderness. Abram had also taken his father into the caravan, knowing he would not return. He would honor the old man until his death several years later.

Lot swayed in the saddle ahead of her. She thought of the rumors she had heard about Lot. He did not seem to share his uncle's passion for treating others with respect. She stirred uneasily, thinking of the young men who had pelted Lot's camel with stones. The animal had muttered and increased the pace, struggling to outrun its tormentors even as Lot had screamed at the men to cease their abuse.

They had spent several years in Haran until Abram's father had died. Then they moved on, following the herds of animals that symbolized the wealth of her husband and his nephew. Years had passed and one longing haunted their lives. She had not become pregnant. She had not given her husband an heir, a son to carry on when Abraham, in turn, became an old man.

She flushed at the thought. All their wealth, all the respect that Abraham carried and yet no son. When the tribal leaders gathered, they asked after Abram's health and the well-being of his children.

What children? Sarai had to admit she was ashamed that she had failed her husband. At least, that was the view of the old chieftains.

Abram reminded her of God's promise of descendants equal to the stars of the sky. How was that to happen when she could not even give him one child, one son?

She had noticed the glances of the serving women around their camp as Abram had walked through the tents. He still walked upright with a strong stride. His skin may have creased in the harsh climate but he remained a man of confidence with the ability to make the difficult decisions. She knew several of the girls tried to catch his eye, thinking they might take her place in his bed. And so, the seed of an idea had been planted.

One morning as she supervised the meal preparation, Hagar, her servant, had stepped forward. There was nothing out of place in the servant's action. She simply came into Sarai's consideration. Hagar's skin gleamed with the oil she had spread over her arms and face. Her dark hair was neatly woven and bound back from her forehead, her nose creating a sharp profile as it sloped down her face. Her bearing was erect, full of confidence. As she swayed through camp, her attitude seemed to proceed her, parting a path through animals and people alike. She was in the prime of her life, ready to bear a child.

Abram had been kind to Sarai. She knew many men took second, even third or fourth wives. The first wife of their youth did not share their beds but became overseers of the family. Yet, Abram honored her as his only wife, even without the gift of children. She didn't want to share his affection, certainly not with this Egyptian! Yet, she thought, Abram needed an heir. Hagar passed by her once again. The woman was striking if not beautiful.

Yes, thought Sarai. Hagar would be strong in childbirth, giving Abraham a healthy son. She pushed the regret aside and rose to find Abram.

"You've seen Hagar, my servant?" she asked him.

"What of her?" replied Abram, smiling, teasing her.

"She is strong and very good to look at!"

"I hadn't noticed," he replied. "You are the one I look at."

"Abram, I've failed you. Over twenty-five years and no son to carry on after you."

"Sarai, we will wait on God. He has promised."

"He has promised that you will have a son. He did not say that it would come from me."

Abram shook his head, saying nothing.

"Your brother sleeps with more than one wife. Between Milpah and his second, he has several children."

"I am aware of my brother's family," said Abram stiffly. "We should talk of something else."

"No. I'm willing to give you Hagar."

"Your maidservant?" asked Abram in surprise.

Sarai said nothing, looking down at the ground.

"Sarai, we will wait for God."

"Take her," she said stiffly. "I believe you may have children through her. We will raise them together."

"You have been my wife all these years. Remember how in Egypt when I watched the Pharoah take you away. I thought I could never look at the man again. I had to pretend as if it was a great honor to offer him my sister."

Sarai laughed softly. "Sister!"

"You don't want this," said Abram. "Wait."

~~~

That evening and the next evening, Sarai watched Hagar as she worked around the camp. The woman moved with arrogance as if she was slightly better than these desert shepherds. But she was healthy and still able to bear children. Finally, she called Hagar to her.

"This evening, take a bath. You will then go to Abram. I am giving you to him to bear his children."

Startled, Hagar had stared briefly at Sarai. She said nothing, waiting for Sarai to explain.

"Go!"

Hagar hurried away. And within a month she was pregnant. She had waited until she was certain, until her middle began to expand, before she had told Abram. He had flushed in expectation. That night, he had motioned for the serving girls to give her the choicest cut of meat.

"You will need to keep up your strength. Child bearing is difficult."

Startled, Sarai had looked rapidly from Abram to Hagar.

"She is with child? Already?"

And Hagar had giggled. She knew this was not the best reaction in front of her mistress but she was the one who now bore a child. A baby, the one her mistress could not give this man. Eagerly, she bit into the meat as the juice squirted across her chin, dripping onto the ground. She watched Sarai.

That evening, there had been no question as to who would sleep with Abram. She had walked to his tent, confident of her place. Sarai, sitting outside her own tent, looked away.

Abram should have foreseen the mounting enmity between the two women. Sarai wanted to believe, when she first offered Hagar, that she would remain Abram's chosen one. But it seemed, as she watched her husband and that woman, that he had begun to give Hagar the best of everything.

How could this have happened, she thought. This is a serving woman, my servant. I am Abram's wife. I have stood by him through times of conflict, through many miles up and down this land. We have loved each other. And now he favors that woman. I never meant for her to replace me in my husband's affection.

"Pick up that rug and shake it," she snapped at Hagar as she entered the tent.

"I am pregnant. Lifting that heavy rug is too hard." Hagar stood back, rubbing her belly as she smiled at her mistress.

What insolence, Sarah thought. There was a time when she would have jumped to obey because she knew I could sell her to the traders. She knows I can do nothing of the kind since she carries Abram's child! Sarai kicked a pot of water nearby.

"At least you can clean up this mess," she said as small rivulets of water tracked through the dust.

"What a waste," declared Hagar. She stepped from the tent and summoned a young girl. "Clean up the rugs and hang them to dry."

"I didn't ask her to do this," snapped Sarai. "I told you."

"I am pregnant with Abram's child."

The two women stared at each other as several servants pretended to be busy, intently watching from under lowered eyelids.

Hagar laughed and turned away. "I do not have to do what you order. I sleep with Abram."

When Abram returned to the camp, Sarai screamed at him in frustration.

"You have placed that woman over me. You made her pregnant and now she thinks she is better than me."

"You gave her to me," Abram offered in defense.

"I didn't think you would treat her as your wife. Now she defies me."

Abram studied his wife as an angry flush crept over her face.

"What happened, Sarai?"

"When I give her an order, she refuses to do what I've said. She thinks herself better than me because she carries your child."

Abram looked out across the camp. Hagar stood in the open, her back straight, arms crossed as she watched the confrontation. He could have sworn she smirked at Sarai's frustration but it might have been nothing more than a shadow. He sighed deeply.

"Once again, I would remind you that this was your idea. And now you are angry with this girl. And with me."

"Only because you treat her as if she is special, more special than the one who has served you, who has followed you all these years." Tears began to rise in her eyes. She angrily turned her face away from Abram. "I won't allow her to treat me with such disrespect, Abram!"

"Do what you want with her." Abram shrugged and turned away. He missed the look that crossed Sarai's face as she stared across the camp at Hagar.

Sarai was careful. Her abuse did not leave marks on the woman. She threw Hagar out of Abram's tent and sent her to work with the girls tending the flocks. At first, Hagar strode along, showing a complete indifference to her mistress. As her belly expanded, her stride became more tentative.

"Hurry out there!" Sarai called to the young woman. "Do you think we have all day to prepare the evening meal?"

Hagar, exhausted, was sent to serve the meal to the men. She stopped briefly in front of Abram, staring down at him. He looked at her and shrugged.

"You once cared for me, for this child," she murmured.

"When the child is born, you will no longer serve in the fields," he replied. "You will be back in camp."

"At least in the fields I do not hear her torment."

Abram turned away to speak with one of his shepherds.

"Hagar! Leave Abram alone to eat his meal," cried Sarai. "Go back to the sheep!"

"Go," whispered Hagar. "She is very good at telling me to go."

Hagar
Genesis 16:7-14

At first, no one noticed her absence. Sunlight spread across the camp, first lighting the tents, then the dusty plain, highlighting the fine grains of dust in the air. The serving girls began to stir, stretching to greet the morning. They blew on the coals of the fire and scooped up handfuls of flour to make little cakes for the first meal of the day.

Sarai sighed in relief, glad that the first face she encountered was not the one she had come to hate. All too soon, the girls called to her, informing her that Hagar was not in the camp.

"What do you want me to do?" she asked. "If Hagar decides to go for a walk, am I supposed to attend her?"

None of them answered her, each failed to meet her gaze. They had all been witness to the growing tension between the two women. With her new status, Hagar had not been a favorite among the other women.

Hagar stumbled again. As she moved forward, the dirt beneath her feet seemed to push rocks and twigs to the surface, catching her toe. Her legs felt as if large weights had been attached, requiring so much effort to lift each foot moving forward. She tried desperately to swallow, her mouth lacking saliva. Heat waves danced across the horizon, leaving Hagar uncertain of the shimmering images caught by her blurry vision. Her skin was hot without the gleam of sweat that would cool her rising temperature.

She stumbled once again. The effort to move forward was almost more than she could summon. She struggled to focus on the ground at her feet. But, no, she must look ahead for some sort of shelter where she could rest until she felt she could move on.

Sarai! That evil woman! Sarai had sent her into the desert with her cruel treatment. She would run and not be troubled again by that woman's spite. But this move might cost her life. She knew without shelter and without water she might not reach safety.

The dry water-skin hung flaccidly from her waist. She had drained the last drop two hours ago. Her tongue, swollen and dry, nearly choked her as she tried to swallow against the rising bile. Too late. She retched, falling forward on her hands and knees. The spittle hung from her lips, dropping into the dirt. She stared at it a moment, disoriented, watching a pattern form in the dust. Gingerly, she touched the design with her forefinger, before falling forward.

No! She must rise, she must move forward. Hagar lay another moment, savoring the opportunity to be still, to be miserable. Then she pushed upward to her knees and hands, stumbling to her feet. One more step; the effort was so very difficult.

A few more yards and she fell once again. Hagar squinted against the sun. The pattern of twigs and leaves shimmered in the light. She crept forward, seeking the shade of the bush.

"Sarai," she whimpered. "You win."

Eyes closed, Hagar lay in the dirt, savoring the relief from her effort, the stillness surrounding her racing heart. Why had she run? Her anger and desperation had driven her out of the camp. She grimaced at the thought. Maybe she hadn't been quite that desperate. Dying alone in the wilderness could be worse than the treatment she had received from Sarai. But, Sarai was the one who had given her to Abram.

She had no right to treat me so badly, thought Hagar. I will die here. No one will find me. She moaned as another wave of nausea swept over her.

She wasn't sure when she first became aware of the silent form standing over her. When she opened her eyes, he stood, staring down at her. The cry of alarm froze in her throat. His regal presence silenced her. She was without defense, unable to form a plea for mercy, an objection to all the accusations that seem to flow her way. She lay there, waiting. Waiting to die at the hand of this stranger. She was not prepared for his first words.

"Do not be alarmed. I will not harm you." He gently lifted her, offering a skin of water.

How could he have known the fear that she had held these past weeks, all at the hands of Sarai? She had wondered if she would survive the labor of childbirth if caught by the pain while working out in the fields. When she lay in deep fatigue, she had wondered how she could rise to answer Sarai's call. Now, she was dying under a bush in the wilderness. Yet, this stranger assured her that she would come to no harm.

~~~

Word spread quickly across the encampment. Hagar had returned. Some said she looked half dead as she hobbled through the tents. After she recovered from the ordeal, a couple of servants thought they saw a difference in her.

Something about Hagar had changed. The servants talked of how the desert could age a woman beyond her time. She had aged. More than years, she seemed to have deeply considered her role and returned, resigned to her fate.

She had returned to her tasks but often stared across the plain as if looking for someone to come. Ignoring Sarai, she seldom answered the commands directed at her. She simply complied with what was asked.

For Hagar, one thought remained. Death had drawn near as she struggled against the wilderness. She had been sent back to her tormentor rather than being allowed to die. God had promised to preserve her, making another great nation from the child she carried. Two nations, at war with each other in the same land. Two nations, one father. This struggle all came down to one man. Abram.

Ishmael
Genesis 16:15-17

How could one man be torn by such conflict and still feel so much joy, wondered Abram. The day Hagar had slipped into labor, he had waited for the announcement. Would it be a son? Possibly a daughter? The old midwife had predicted a son based on her superstitions. He thought no one could know until the child emerged to take the first breath. When the moment came, he had seemed to receive the birth of a son calmly but his mind silently soared at the announcement.

Sarai sat nearby, watching his reaction. She remained uneasy around Hagar. He would not add to her torment, he thought, by making too much of the child. But a son! The child was a boy! He turned his face to gaze out across the land, hiding his elation from Sarai.

"Abram!" Sarai spoke sharply. "I know you rejoice in the birth of a son. Don't hide it from me."

He turned to watch her a moment, seeking to know whether she could tolerate the joy that filled him. Sarai turned to a serving girl.

"Bring the child to his father. We would see the child."

"Sarai, I love you no less." He turned to her. "Believe that, even as I rejoice at the birth of my son. Someday, God will give us a child."

"Abram," Sarai scoffed. "I am old. This is your son of the promise."

"No, I believe there will be another son, born to us. God has promised."

As the servant girl approached with the baby, Sarai rose to her feet. She stared down into the face of the baby.

"He has his mother's nose."

"He is a fine son!" said the girl. "The women say he bellowed as he came from his mother."

Abram laughed as Sarai snorted in disgust.

"It seems he takes after his mother in more than appearance. She is always the first to complain about her tasks," she said.

The girl glanced quickly at Abram, gauging his reaction to the criticism. Abram stared at the child, seeming to be unaware of Sarai's comments.

"Take him back to his mother. He needs her now." Abram turned away, ignoring Sarai as she placed a hand on his arm. "I will be with the herdsmen."

How could one man contain such joy, wondered Abram. The joy only lasted a short time before the antagonism between Hagar and Sarai had broken out once again.

"Abram! That woman is telling the girls that she does not have to serve me."

"That woman?" He turned to look at Sarai.

"You know I mean Hagar."

"Sarai! She has a baby to look after. Don't be so hard on her."

"You think I'm hard on her?"

"I think you long for a child. Your day will come. Patience, Sarai. God has promised."

"This has nothing to do with a child. This is about respect, Abram."

He said nothing, watching her. She broke off and looked back at him uneasily. Had she pushed him too far? Why didn't he listen to her, she wondered.

Abram, watched her, thinking how beautiful she remained. Her hair was now streaked with gray. The lines around her eyes creased white against the deep tan that stained her skin. But her eyes remained so bright, just as they had appeared when she stared up at him in the marketplace.

"Sarai, do you remember the day we met, in the marketplace?"

Her gazed shifted but the tension in her jaw eased slightly. After a moment, she nodded, just once.

"Sarai, with the all the years between us, you mean more to me than any other woman. God has promised a great nation that will come from a son born to you and I. Not just me. I cannot bear a child. You will be the mother of a great nation."

Sarai didn't respond. She stared out across the plain. Abram waited, willing her to relax from the tension that filled her.

"I would never have consented to take Hagar as the mother of my child if I had thought of the tension this would cause between us. You asked me to take her but I regret that choice. We did not wait for God to act as he promised."

Sarai shifted her weight uneasily.

"Abram, I regret asking you to conceive a child with Hagar. But I am too old to have a child. What choice did we have?"

"To wait, to trust God."

Tears swelled in Sarai's eyes.

"Abram, I don't wish to think of this. We are caught in the present. We cannot undo the past."

"No. Ishmael is from me and with him a part of me will remain. A part I can never retrieve. The presence of the boy reminds me of the lack of faith I would redeem."

"Redeem? You would take back what you've given?"

"I won't renounce my son, Sarai. He remains in the camp. What would you have me do?"

Silent, Sarai shook her head and turned away.

"And so, we wait," she said. "We have failed to produce a child, we have failed to trust God. What is left?"

"To wait, to trust that God will do as he promised."

The Second Son
Genesis 18:1-15

As the light began to dim, three visitors appeared on the horizon, making their way toward the camp. Abraham rose from his seat beneath the ancient trees that marked Mamre. He graciously invited the three men to sit while the women moved to quickly prepare food and drink for the visitors.

His dark eyes examined the three men, their clothing, their bearing as they moved confidently into the shade of the trees to settle on rugs spread over the dusty ground. Abraham called for water, offering the men refreshment in washing the dust from their feet, hands and faces. The women kneaded bread dough near stone ovens. The bawling of a calf was cut short as the blood flowed from its severed veins. Servants soon roasted large cuts of meat for the evening meal. Abraham offered his visitors a traditional drink, whey curds swirling in creamy milk, from the goat herds that drifted through distant pastures.

Abraham watched his visitors carefully, aware that they were not from a neighboring locale. His eldest servants could remember the solid mud structures of Haran, the town that last sheltered Abraham before he embarked on a journey to this remote plain. He had been relatively well off by the standards of his community. Then, he claimed that a Spirit, unseen by human eyes, was ordering him to leave the mud bricks behind for a nomadic life in a tent. He was to follow great herds of sheep and goats. This Spirit had promised to make his descendants a great nation, powerful throughout the earth. Those that cursed his descendants would find the curse returned upon them. He knew he had stood in the presence of the Almighty God

The visitors began to speak with Abraham, drawing his attention back to their presence.

"Do you remember the time when you came to this land?"

"Yes, we came from Haran. A long journey. In those days, I was known as Abram."

"And what drew you to this plain?"

"I was summoned."

"What do you know of the one who summoned you?"

"He does not exist as a man and yet he created all that man sees and knows. There was a time when he spoke with me. First, in Ur, then in Haran. There was a time when he came out of the darkness. He made a covenant with me."

"A covenant? Do you bear the mark of this covenant?"

"Just as we divide each animal in half when we make a covenant, so God required an incision of my flesh and that of my son and male servants as the sign of our covenant. I was ninety-nine years of age when the my blood and flesh sealed this covenant. With this covenant, he changed my name and the name of my wife, Sarah. I am now called Abraham."

Breaking free from his reminiscing, Abraham watched the visitors taste his bread, the sizzling roast placed before them. But he sensed that hospitality was not their goal in visiting his camp.

With the meal consumed, one of the men inquired as to Abraham's health. "God has blessed me with good health," he replied, still waiting.

"And Sarah, where is she?" the visitor asked.

Abraham could hear the slightest giggle from one of Sarah's helpers. "She is back in the tent," he said, nodding at the dusty form rising toward the branches above. He could imagine how Sarah strained to hear the mention of her name.

"When I return next year, she will have given you a son." The visitor smiled, watching Abraham struggle between elation and doubt. Turning his head slightly to look at the tent, the visitor asked, "Why does Sarah laugh? Why does she believe that this is too hard for God?"

Hidden in the tent, Sarah cringed back against the rugs. She had not made a sound. Amusement filled her at the visitor's words. How could he have known that she silently laughed at this announcement. She was too old to become pregnant. Even if the father had been a young man from among Abraham's servants, her body had betrayed her. She no longer bled monthly. Her time was past. Fear crept into her. How could this visitor have heard her doubt, unspoken but creasing throughout her consciousness?

Genesis 21:1-6

Six months later, Sarah came to him, gripping his arm. In her excitement, her nails dug painfully into the fragile skin that covered his forearm.

"Abraham!"

Something about her voice caused him to turn and look at her for a long moment. Her skin was flushed. He had not seen this vitality in many years from her, yet she glowed. He laughed.

"You look young today. What has you so excited?"

"Abraham, you will not believe this! I think I am certain."

He waited, smiling. "Are you going to tell me what has you so excited."

She grabbed his hand, pressing it against her abdomen. He pulled back sharply and then looked at her once again.

"Yes," she nodded.

Slowly, he extended his hand once again, his eyebrows raised as he gently touched her.

"Yes," she breathed. "I'm an old woman but I carry a child."

She clung to him and he supported her weight for a moment as they both remembered the visit six months earlier of three visitors.

"Our visitors spoke of a child. How could they have known I would carry a child when I am so far along in years?" she asked.

"They were not men such as I," he replied. "But this is

possible. He promised."

"So, we are not so old. Remember that one night?"

Abraham threw back his head and joyfully laughed. Others around the camp turned and watched them, wondering what had caused their master such joy.

The years of passion had faded, no longer did they come together with the urgency of their younger years. Given time, touching, slowly moving together, they could create a closeness that gave way to ardor, a longing for physical completion as husband and wife. One night those early days had seemed to come alive for a few moments as Abraham gasped in passion, binding her closely to his aging body. Afterward, they had laughed at how for that moment they chased the echoes of their youth.

Twenty-five years he had toiled, herding his flocks. Twenty-five years of pacing this desert land, bound by Egypt to the south, Mesopotamia to the north. Looking for springs, he had searched out good pasture, moving on when his flocks had eaten all the earth would give them for a time.

Abraham wondered, as the time grew close, whether his wife would be able to endure the struggle, the physical demands of childbirth. The hours of labor were not easy for a young woman. Would the struggle to expel this screaming infant from her womb, deplete an old woman, draining her of life? Would he mourn one even as he celebrated the other? Would he lose both child and wife in one brief moment?

Sarah had wakened one morning, close to her time, complaining of the dull pain stretching across her lower back. After exchanging a long look with the midwife, she had drifted around the encampment, stopping to clutch her middle as the pain increased to engulf her rounded belly. With each contraction, her face tightened in pain. Her gray hair dampened with the beads of sweat that began to trace a course along her temples. She did not complain.

The midwife set out the birthing stool and her tools before she swept Sarah into the tent where she would be secluded for the next few days. Sarah's servants crept in and out as the hours moved past and the cries of their mistress issued from the dwelling. The midwife knew her job and she never ceased her effort to ease the entry of the child into the camp of the living.

At last, she thrust the knife through the umbilical cord as Sarah wondrously stroked the tiny male child. The midwife bound the baby in strips of cloth before returning him to his mother.

"At last," breathed Sarah. "I am a wife. I am a mother, giving him a child."

The women of the camp pressed forward, each examining the small hands and feet, the tiny ears and nose, the dark eyes that turned intently toward each voice celebrating his arrival. Abraham could scarcely contain his impatience, pacing the camp. He longed to see the promised child. The one who would fulfill the covenant with God.

One of the servants finally slipped from the tent and quietly approached the old man. The men around him, busy with their tasks, pretended not to notice. Each one silently observed her approach, watching for his reaction.

He exploded upward as if the years had dropped away. Thrusting his fist into the air, he cried for all to hear.

"A son!"

His men surged forward to congratulate him as if nothing could be more important than this moment in their lives. Abraham dropped to the ground, stumbling as he landed. One servant caught him and then pulled back, embarrassed that he had brought attention to his master's weakness.

"A son! God, a son!" Abraham cried. He sank to his knees, his face raised to the heavens. Tears leaked from the corners of his eyes. Then he was on his feet again, surging toward the women's tent.

"I would see him!"

The midwife met him at the door. "Not now, wait a bit."

A servant swept past with bloody cloths and Abraham fell back, his eyes on the blood. Suddenly, the reality of Sarah's labor struck him. This was her blood. He turned to the midwife, his eyebrows raised.

"Yes, she lives. She will be fine. Both of them are fine. You will see them."

On the eighth day, he lifted his son upward before the eyes of those in the encampment, proclaiming, "This is God's promise."

He sliced through the skin covering the tiny penis as the child wailed his protest against the unexpected assault. His tiny fists flailed against the emptiness around him before his nurse swept him up to comfort the husky cries.

"He will be called Isaac," Abraham announced to the

men and women who served him.

Slowly, they began to mutter, "Laughter? Why laughter?"

Abraham watched their reaction, a little smile crossing his own lips. When he had finally been allowed to enter the tent, Sarah had reached for him.

"You've seen him?" she asked.

He smiled, bending over her to stroke back a strand of gray hair that fell along her cheek.

"Yes! You've given me a son. God has fulfilled his promise to us."

A slight flush covered her tired face.

"His promise," she muttered. "I thought such a promise could never happen to an old woman. Here I am, a mother. Who would have said that I, Sarah, would give you a son."

He laughed. "Not so unusual for an old man but I am deeply blessed."

"I laughed when our visitor said I would bear a child!"

"We need to give him a name that reminds us and others of God's blessing." He suddenly laughed, filled with exuberance over his son. "We could name him laughter."

"Abraham!" The flush on Sarah's face deepened. But then she laughed.

"God has brought me laughter and all who hear of this boy will laugh with me. Yes! The tears are gone. We celebrate with laughter!'

Cast Out
Genesis 22:1-3

One child, his son, the fulfillment of a promise. This was just the beginning of a line of descendants of one man. Abraham stumbled over a rocky impression, catching himself before he could drop to the ground.

"Father!" Isaac bounded forward to grasp his father's arm. "Watch your step!"

Amused, Abraham gazed down at the young man.

"Do you think I am that old?" he asked. "I would break in two from a slight stumble?"

"Uh, I . ." Isaac struggled to put words to his concern without offending his aging father. "I hate to see you fall."

Abraham wrapped his arm around his son's shoulder as they moved forward. He leaned forward slightly as Isaac braced himself against the pressure.

Isaac smiled at this father, saying nothing. But he held himself to his father's pace, without bounding away to chase the donkey that bore their food. He could leave that to his father's men.

Abraham watched his son as he gazed out across the

landscape. The boy had grown strong, full of life. Now, as they traveled north to Hebron and beyond, to Mount Moriah, the miles seem to slog by under his feet.

Isaac, God's promise fulfilled.

He had waited so long, believing that God would do what he had said. And now, would God take his son from him?

Abraham could see a smudge of green on the horizon. He knew that as they drew closer, the great trees at Mamre would rise from the line between earth and sky to dominate the attention of any man crossing this dry land. He had camped at the springs when he traveled south from his homeland years before. He had returned since then to camp in their shade, a relief from the exposure to the intense sun.

"Father! I see the trees of Mamre!"

Isaac raised his arm, pointing toward the smudge.

"Yes, Mamre!"

"Is that where we're going?" asked his son eagerly.

Abraham shook his head.

"Much farther. We will stop the night at Mamre and then move on in the morning."

Isaac raced forward toward the men with the donkeys.

"We stop at Mamre!"

The men smiled at him.

"A good place to stop. Your father is well-respected by the chieftain in this region."

Isaac studied the men for a moment.

"How does this man know my father?"

"Years ago, they met when your father came down from Haran. Your father has great flocks of goats and sheep. The chieftain knows that God blesses him."

"The chieftain knows God?"

Both men laughed.

"No, he sees the flocks of sheep and goats. He knows your father is a wealthy man and a valuable ally."

Abraham listened to the conversation. What would become of the flocks if Isaac was no longer with him? He thought of God's command. His feet stopped moving. Weakness swept the strength from his legs. He thought he might collapse to the ground.

"God! Not this son. You promised an heir. You promised a son. He is here. How could you take him when he is the fulfillment of the promise?"

"Trust!"

He heard the word echo through his mind. God was asking if he, Abraham, could trust him. Anguish filled Abraham.

"Not this boy," he thought. "God, he is all I have. I cannot bear for you to take him."

"Trust! Do you trust me to know what is best?"

"God, look at him. How strong he is. How he listens to my men. He is my dearest treasure and you demand him. Haven't I served you all these years, faithful to your demands."

"Trust? Do you trust me to keep my promise?"

"But God, you did keep that promise. He stands right here. How can you take him?"

Isaac, turned to check on his father. Abraham stood still, shrinking into the robes that hung from his gaunt frame. Why didn't he move forward? He was the one to declare a camp at Mamre.

"Father! Are you all right?"

Abraham waved him forward and staggered another few feet. The boy watched him, examining his movements.

"God, he knows I am not right in my mind. He knows I am troubled. Surely, you do not intend what you ask. Deliver him!"

The answer came more softly.

"Who planted the great trees of Mamre? Do you see them up ahead?"

Abraham squinted into the glare coming off the desert. He refused to answer, waiting for the next thought to swirl through his mind.

"Have you seen the great sea? Yes? Who dug its depths. Who caused the waves to surge up on the land? Where were you at the moment of creation?

"But God, this is my son. The one you gave me, the one you promised."

"Who caressed the mountain goat into existence? Their sharp hooves tapping against the rock ledges are music to my ears."

"Isaac's laughter is my music. Don't take him!"

God was silent. Abraham struggled to lift his foot for another step.

"I cannot let him go!"

There was no response.

"God, do not be silent now!" wailed Abraham. Suddenly, he realized he had spoken aloud. He glanced quickly ahead. Had they heard him? Isaac and his companions strode along as if nothing broke the silence.

~~~

Genesis 21:8-21

Silence! He longed for silence once. Hagar and Sarah had squabbled over every little matter. He could hardly remember a time when the camp had been torn by such tension as it was when Isaac made his appearance.

He had leaped for joy. A son! The son of God's promise. The tiny baby stretched out his hand, his arm flexing against the unexpected freedom. Sunlight flooded the tiny form as his son seemed to bathe in its warmth. He stretched again, testing his limbs, unbound from the womb, no longer restrained by strips of cloth. Abraham laughed at his cautious exploration as Isaac now extended a foot.

"That's right, my boy. We've broken free of the women who keep you so confined."

He turned to see Sarah looking on. Her smile illuminated the contentment shining in her eyes.

"God is faithful," he reminded her.

A sob broke from her throat. She nodded silently, unwilling to speak.

Abraham lifted his son against his chest.

"Look!" He commanded. "We are foreigners here. We will always wander the land. But from you, a people will come to take the best of the land set before you!"

Isaac pitched forward as Abraham caught him with his free hand.

"Abraham!"

"I caught him, Sarah! We were just checking the flocks."

"The flocks are miles away. Be careful!"

Abraham smiled, the creases of his face deepening. He stroke the tiny baby, whispering in his ear.

"You are the promise. All of this will come to your descendants, to our people. God is faithful."

A twig snapped and Abraham turned his head to stare at Ishmael. The boy quickly tossed a stone across the small wadi at the edge of camp.

"Ishmael! What are you doing?" called Abraham.

The boy acted as if he didn't hear his father. He slid down the embankment.

"I don't like how he acts around Isaac!" said Sarah.

"He is just a little boy! In a few years, he won't be around much. He'll be out with the herds."

"A little boy who seems to have too much free time! I've caught him teasing Isaac. He pinches him when he thinks no one is looking!"

"Sarah! He is just a boy. What harm can he really do?"

It was not the last time, Sarah would complain about Ishmael, thought Abraham. She seemed to hold a grudge against the boy. As Isaac took his first steps, Ishmael seemed to be around less often. But one day, as Abraham returned to camp, Sarah hurried toward him.

"You must send Hagar and Ishmael away!"

"Send them from the camp?"

"Yes, I will not have that boy tormenting Isaac!"

"Sarah, they are boys. You must get used to a little rough play. Boys do that!"

"Abraham, that boy wasn't playing when he tripped your son this afternoon. When Isaac began to cry, Ishmael slapped him!"*

Abraham sent for Ishmael but he seemed to have disappeared into the brush surrounding the camp. In just a week, Isaac would be weaned from nursing. He would begin to take his place in the rhthym of the camp, learning small chores. Abraham pondered the tension between his two sons.

Was Sarah right in demanding that Ishmael be sent away? He fell asleep as he considered the tension between the two women and their sons.

God spoke in the dream that stole through his sleep-addled brain.

"Isaac is the son of the promise."

As consciousness returned, he understood what must happen.

"Send Hagar to me!" he called.

She came with a smile, a bounce in her step. He realized that he had not sent for her in months. She must be expecting some pleasant surprise.

"Hagar!"

Her face tightened as she looked at him.

"What? You didn't want me to come?"

---

* Genesis 21:9

"No, I called for you. We must talk about your son."

"Ishmael. He is growing so tall! Aren't you pleased with him?"

"Hagar, God promised a son to me. I have that promise in Isaac."

A sullen look stole over her face.

"And my son? What of him? He is your son, too!"

"God has promised that he will become a great nation."

Relief replaced the sullen look.

"Yes! From our son, a great nation."

"In time, yes. But now, he must go. He is not the son of the promise, the one that God has blessed. I am sending him away."

"Away? How are we to survive?"

"I will give you provisions."

"This is Sarah's doing! She is jealous of Ishmael!"

"No, not Sarah. I am sending you and Ishmael away. He will not receive the inheritance promised to Isaac."

"Abraham, he is your son."

"Yes, my son. But not the one promised by God. He came in a moment of weakness when I failed to wait on God. Now he must be sent from the camp."

"But I came back! I came back because God sent me back. You remember when I ran from Sarah? God sent me back."

"God tells me Ishmael must be sent away. In the morning, I will give you provisions. You will take your son and follow the road to the south."

Hagar stood erect, glaring at Abraham. In one swift

movement, she spat on the ground at Abraham's feet and then turned to stride away.

Months after their departure, word reached him. Two merchants had seen a young man skinning his catch, near a desert well. When they asked after his family, he had given the name of Abraham as his father.

"Is he well?" asked Abraham.

The merchants shifted uneasily.

"He is well, a skilled archer for one so young. He claims to have been cast off and nearly died as his mother wandered in the desert."

Abraham listened impassively, wondering how much they knew. His son would live as God had promised. But he would live at enmity with the descendants of Isaac.

"God, what of my son? How could I have been so slow to wait on you?"

~~~

His memories faded as the men moved into the shade. Abraham eased to the ground under one tree. He watched Isaac dipped a water skin into the well. Cool water, dripped from the bag as the men lifted it over the rocks edging the deep hole.

"Isaac!" he groaned. "One son gone. Now you would have the other as well? What of your promise?

Isaac

Awake in the early hours before dawn, his memory pulled Abraham back through the years to a lambing season. Isaac pushed through the milling sheep, corralled by a stone wall.

"I've found three more ewes, just dropped," he told his father. Their lambs are up and nursing well."

"Three more healthy lambs! This is a good year."

"I'm so tired I think I could drop and sleep right here."

Abraham smiled at his son and reached out to massage one of his shoulders.

"You're a great help to the shepherds during lambing season. We need every hand we can get and you do more than your share for one so young."

"I like this time of year, seeing the lambs drop. I enjoy watching the lambs play around the ewes. We work into exhaustion but every lamb increases our herds."

"This has been a better year," agreed Abraham. "We lost too many to the drought last year. I'll be glad to see these lambs thrive."

One of the shepherds stumbled over with a small, still form in his arms. "Another for the predators I'm afraid. We just didn't get to this one in time."

"We were just saying this was a good year. Take the carcass well past the hills. We don't want to encourage the wolves to move down into the flocks. We're busy enough with lambing without having to send extra men to patrol the outskirts of the flocks."

"I had better make another circuit," said Isaac. "If I had been more vigilant, we might have saved that one."

"Don't take one loss personally. We lose a few each year. Go see your mother for a bite to eat and then get some sleep."

"I can stay up a little longer,"

"Isaac, you are more precious to me than all my herds. We have good men working with us. I trust them but you are the chosen one."

Isaac smiled at Abraham. "Seems I've heard that as long as I can remember."

"Decades for me. Since you were born."

"I only want to prove myself as good as any of our shepherds. I know what my heritage brings me. Better I learn it now while you are still with us."

"You have proven yourself, Isaac. God has given me a son I am proud of."

Father and son watched the sheep moving restlessly. Many were yet to birth their lambs and the shepherds kept a close watch for ewes that were drawing close to their time. Once one started, she inspired all the rest to follow. The men worked long hours, ensuring that each lamb rose to his feet and found his mother. By the end of the lambing season, the men would crawl into their beds, swearing they could sleep for a month. As Isaac laughed at a lamb's antics, Abraham seemed to stir himself from deep thought, turning toward his son. He broke their silence.

"Traders came by yesterday."

"I thought I saw the dust of a caravan approaching the camp."

"We did well trading our stock for cotton goods, some delicacies from the south. They seemed pleased with the animals we offered."

"They were returning to Egypt?"

"Shortly. They brought news along with the trade goods."

"News of Egypt?"

"Of Ishmael. He has taken a wife. Hagar found a wife for him in Egypt."[*]

"May God bless him with many sons!"

Abraham laughed. "God has promised to bless both of you. From the time he called me from Ur, God named me the father of a great nation. That nation is to come through you. But then you've heard me say that many times."

"God, the creator of heaven and earth. How can we know His timing, the fulfillment of His promises?"

"One is standing right in front of me. His promise was fulfilled in your birth."

"Yes, I understand that but for now it is enough to think of the next ewe to tremble as her lamb breaks free."

"Isaac, never deny God's promise."

[*] Genesis 21:21

"Never! I believe him. Time trickles slowly for his promises unlike when lambing season breaks loose."

Abraham chuckled. "You are ready for a few hours of sleep. Go! Find your mother. She undoubtably has a meal for you."

"Isaac! Come hold this nanny for me so her kid can suckle," yelled one of the shepherds as he braced himself, clutching the horns of a large female goat. Frantically, the nanny twisted, bleating her protest at being handled so brusquely.

Isaac laughed and waved his father away.

"I can catch a little sleep after I help hold this nanny. I'll see you tonight."

His memories filled the wakeful hours. Now sleep eluded him as Abraham stared into the darkness. He braced his hips against the hard ground, turning to seek a more comfortable position.

How could God fulfill his promise of a son and then ask for him back? His God was not in the form of the fiery god of the Canaanites, thought Abraham. He called his people to live righteously, promising great rewards for their obedience. When had God ever asked for a sacrifice of a child?

"This is the child you once promised. How can you ask me to sacrifice him as one of my lambs?"

"Trust me."

"No! My son is not a lamb to slice open and serve for dinner. He is a breathing, loving young man, the joy of my life. His spirit was created by your hand. How can you ask me to press a knife to his throat, to shed his blood?"

"Trust me," God whispered.

"And what of your promise? How will you raise up a nation from this child if I slay him?"

"Do you not trust me to know what is best for your son?"

"I have followed you these many years. I have displayed my trust but I cannot answer that question."

"Do I not love him more than any other man within this land? Have I not promised you great things from him? Trust me."

Abraham slid down to his knees, his face dipping to the dust. He could feel the tears clogging the back of his throat, leaving his breath raspy.

"God, you have asked me to place a knife to his throat, to slice into that living vein. I cannot take the life of one I love so much. How can you ask this?"

"Trust me."

"You ask me to trust you when you would rip away this child I love more than my own life. How can I believe that this is from you and not some evil spirit haunting my dreams?"

"Abraham, how long have we walked together?"

His undergarment clung to his damp skin. His hand cramped from clasping the staff with ancient fingers. He squinted against the darkness, refusing to answer the question, the demand that haunted his mind.

"Why? Why would you take him, the child of the promise? God, I cannot give him up!"

"Abraham, if I should stretch out my hand and steal his breath, how would you stop me? If I should take his life in a moment, could you stand in the way?"

"You know I cannot," replied Abraham. "I can only plead for your mercy, for the life of my son."

"Was it not I who gave you Isaac?"

"Isaac, the gift of laughter," Abraham thought. "The gift of joy. Yes, you gave us this gift. I ask that you spare him."

"We have spoken of this before. I did not spare Sodom and Gomorrah."

"I asked you to spare those towns if you found ten righteous men," said Abraham. "Only Lot and his daughters survived. I stand before you as a man less than righteous. Would you take me as penance and allow my son grow into a man."

"Abraham, I promised a nation from Isaac. Do you trust me to do this?"

"God, I am only a man, with imperfect thoughts. You asked me to sacrifice my son. I can only reply that you are a God who keeps his promises. I remind you of your promise."

As he lay under the trees of Mamre, the black faded into gray across the eastern horizon, Abraham waited for God. He waited to hear the other men begin to stir. The dark hills on either side of the valley formed a corridor that led north to Mount Moriah. Abraham dreaded that moment when he stood at the peak, overlooking the valley below. Would he find God waiting for him or would only the vultures circle that high place, keeping him company?

His men began to stir, rubbing the sleep from their eyes. One rose while the other sat, stretching his arms upward toward the leafy canopy above them. Isaac slept on.

He sleeps like one with a clear conscience, thought Abraham. I find it easier to let him sleep rather than nudge the boy onward. He settled back against a pack as the first rays of sunlight began to pierce the canopy.

The quiet contemplation ended as Isaac stretched across his sleeping pad. Abraham sighed deeply. He knew he could no longer delay the moment of departure. They must begin to pack the animals. He could choose to return the way they had come. No one knew the purpose of this journey. He could simply tell his men to turn back, that he had changed his mind about the purpose of this trip. No one would question his leadership.

He studied the boy as he rose from the pad. Sturdy legs supported his torso with muscles tightening across the ribs. His young face bore no strain from squinting against the harsh glare. His dark hair was tousled and would remain so much of the day until Isaac swiping at rivulets of sweat eased it back across the top of his head.

There was always a choice. He had chosen to listen to the quiet voice in the deep hours of night. He had chosen to sell his possessions, gather his herds and follow the direction of an unseen spirit to this land on the edge of the Great Sea. He had chosen to submit to the knife when God called for the men to slice away the foreskin of their male organs, marking them as his own. He was only a man. He could turn back from this challenge God had placed before him. Would this God forgive such an act. Was it only his own dark thoughts that led him toward Mount Moriah?

The shadow of that whisper echoed through the passages of his mind. "If I should choose to take his life, could you stop me?"

The men bound the packs to the donkeys and fell into an easy pace. They glanced at each other without exchanging comment. The look on each man's face spoke of his concern for Abraham, lost in his thoughts as he walked forward. Isaac was not immune to the concern of his father's men but he refused to buckle under the somber silence that bound the men.

He tossed a small rock at a cedar grove on the hillside below them. Small deer darted from the shade beneath of the trees. A blackbird rose into the sky, heavy wings straining to gain lift in the warm air. Isaac laughed.

"He has found his share of mice. Look at how slow he rises."

Abraham stretched one hand against the glare of the early morning sun to watch the bird's flight. The light flared against the back of hand, illuminating the shadow of the bones beneath the taunt skin. He seemed able to trace the flow of blood through the veins in his hand. Slowly, he flexed the muscles, clenching his hand into a fist. He released the fingers from the tight knot they formed against his palm and watched the light once again pick out the skeletal shadow beneath the skin.

These fingers would grip a knife. This hand would draw the blade in a sweeping arc across Isaac's throat. With a cry, he flung his hand outward as if he would cast it away, disowning it as a traitor to the love he held for his son.

"I cannot do this!" he thought closing his eyes.

"Look!" cried Isaac. "The peak is smoking!"

Abraham's eyes flew open. Ahead of the men, Mount Moriah rose above the foothills. A thin stream of cirrus clouds arced upward from the peak, appearing as a stream of smoke.

"This is the place," God whispered. "I ask you to walk by faith. I ask you to trust me." *

---

* Genesis 22:4

Upon This Peak
Genesis 22:5-9

Abraham stared at the range of hills ahead of his men. He sensed the moment had come, the moment he would step forward into the unknown. He could walk into the future as dark as it appeared. Or he could choose to turn back to the familiar, to the life he had led. Who could say that the joy he had known the last few years would continue if he chose to turn back?

The men pulled their donkeys to a stop and gazed back at the old man hunched across the neck of his animal. One man glanced at the other as if to ask whether they should turn back to check on the old man.

The men had found Abraham to be strangely quiet the last two days. They knew that he often talked with an unseen Presence. In the quiet hours, after the shepherds returned to camp each evening, he would talk to them of this unseen Spirit, the mark of obeisance written across his bent frame.

Slowly, Abraham raised his hand, commanding them to wait as he moved forward. He nodded toward a small grove of trees on the hillside, rising above the trail.

"Wait. Wait here. Isaac and I will go ahead. We will worship. Wait for our return."

The men examined the small grove and then turned to look at him, waiting for further explanation. He offered none. Slowly, he urged his animal forward, beckoning Isaac to move ahead.

Isaac remained silent. Questioning his father could be taken as a lack of respect for the old man. He squinted against the glare, watching the ravines drop from the ridge line down to valley below. If Abraham chose to be quiet, Isaac would wait until his father indicated that he wished to share what he was considering in his silence.

A hare startled from under dense scrub, racing the donkey as they plodded onward. The hare shot off the ridge, into denser brush. Isaac laughed abruptly.

"If I weren't on a journey, you would have been dinner," he called after the hare.

He glanced back at his father. The old man showed no reaction to his son's outburst.

It is strange to see him so morose, thought Isaac. He turned back to the ravine on one side. Pebbles dislodged by the donkey's feet skittered into the void, their descent marked by a snapping sound as they bounced against larger rocks in their descent. Overhead, a raven hung almost motionless, riding the heat waves rising from the desert.

The boy watches the raven, thought Abraham. He sees everything around him and chooses to act based on what he sees.

I have a choice. I can turn back or I can go forward, believing what I cannot see. What do I base this decision on? Do I turn back, afraid of the unknown?

This unseen God called me from Ur. He led me to this land. At least, I believe he led me. He has caused me to prosper. I am wealthier than many of my neighbors. He thought of Mamre, the Amorite, who owning the oasis. We once made a pact to support each other, allowing our shepherds to graze their flocks on each other's pasture. That was a good decision but ultimately, the increase in my flocks became too much for the pasture and water from the wells. Other men have worked just as hard with comparable resources and they have not seen the increase I have been given.

What of that day when the visitors walked into our camp and I learned what would befall Sodom? He grimaced at the thought of the insolent king who had once ruled the destroyed city. At first their dealings had been amiable, but soon enough, he had begun to sense the true nature of the pagan king. On the day of Sodom's destruction, the three visitors to his camp had pulled Lot and his family from the city even as the odor of sulfur reeked through the valley.

And there was Isaac, a child promised long after Sarah had passed through the years of child bearing. Yes, there was that promise fulfilled in the young man who so eagerly strode ahead. All of this was what he could see, touch, smell.

What is the purpose of faith when obedience is absent? thought Abraham. I have obeyed this Spirit's commands and I have seen the results. Each promise, each prediction has come to pass. But even without the security of knowing what would happen, I have chosen to walk forward as the decisions came before me. Faith is not based on guarantees for the future. It is the essence of stepping forward, trusting in a promise. And what purpose would faith serve with a guarantee? No faith would be required if I knew the results before I stepped forward to obey.

I lived by faith and came to see this boy born in my old age. And in faith, he still draws each breath. God has placed his hand over my son and allowed him to prosper just as everything I own has grown in the years that I have walked with this Spirit I know as God.

And now, can I step forward and offer back the fulfillment of God's promise? Can I raise my hand to take the life of my son who I love more than all else? If I were to take his life, what then? What would be left but a corpse?

God asked me to live by faith and faith unfulfilled by action is worthless As worthless as a corpse. Faith is nothing unless I live out every aspect of that belief in my daily routine.

He had watched his neighbors and their empty religious rituals. Was this an expression of faith? Without a doubt. But what did they place their faith in as they threw their children into the fire? Was he not better than those men and women who strove to appease a god represented in a roughly carved tree trunk? Yes, he had been blessed but who was to say that this was not happenstance?

He thought again to the moment when Sarah had dared to hope that she was pregnant with his child. He could not name one other woman that had given birth at such an age as Sarah. The evidence walked the ridge ahead of him. A small spark of hope began to flicker. He roughly pushed it aside. He could not allow himself to move based on an incautious wish. His actions must acknowledge the truth of what he had been called to do.

Faith. Ending in a decomposing corpse. The death of all his dream, the death of a promise. For if Isaac died, what would be left but this Spirit who called for his obedience?

The two men, one with thin white hair, the other approaching his prime, strode along the ridge. To one side, the gullies dropped into a river valley, one of the few sources of water year around. Off to their left, hidden behind another range of hills lay the great sea. This route had been followed by travelers for centuries since the mountains had sunk their roots into the earth's crust. Invading armies had passed along the ridge line, marching north, tramping south, intent on conquering lands beyond their own. Now Abraham stood alone along the highline, a tiny figure under the harsh sun as it baked the desert plains. His spirit was secluded from even his son. He, alone, stood at a crossroads.

His donkey plodded along the trail, its head drooping under the heat that emanated from the rocks. For a moment, one hoof caught in a crevice. The animal stumbled before regaining its footing. Isaac, hearing the clatter, glanced back. He turned to help his father. Abraham pointed down the slope.

"I wouldn't be the first to take a tumble."

Isaac's gaze followed his father's gesture to the hillside

below. Scraps of fur clung to rocks surrounding the remains of a skeleton. A raw gash on the hillside above the bones indicated what had happened weeks earlier. A goat had stepped onto a rocky ledge below the trail, only to have the hillside give way under it's weight.

Passing the site, Abraham thought about the unfortunate animal. Blindly, it had stepped out onto the ledge, believing that the rocks would support its weight. Instead, the rocks had given way before the animal could leap to safety, the body tumbling down the hillside, caught in the rush of boulders.

Now I'm the one contemplating what it means to take a step of faith, thought Abraham. And I could be left with nothing but my son's body to bear home to a heartbroken mother. If I say I believe, I must step out, relying only on a promise.

But why has God asked me to give up the fulfillment of his promise. Even when Ishmael was born, God told me the boy was not the son he had promised. I was content but God gave us Isaac. And now, he asks me to surrender my son.

As the sun passed the zenith of the sky's arc overhead, the men steadily climbed upward, following an ancient trail that led through a range of hills. To either side, low hills formed an escarpment, obstructing the approach to the higher peaks ahead. The summit of Mount Moriah was swept by dry winds, lending a sense of desolation to the peak. Overhead, vultures rode the heated updrafts rising from the plains baking under the merciless sun.

A place of sacrifice, thought Abraham, with the scavengers as sentries for the dead.

"Where are you?" he cried to the Spirit who led him to the peak. "Am I to stand here alone in my grief? Have you forgotten your promise of the nation that will flow across this land below my feet? Where are you?"

Unaware that he had cried aloud, he was startled to see his son turn back to look at him.

"Did you cry out?" Isaac asked. Abraham sighed deeply.

"I did. My spirit is very heavy to be called here."

"Then why have we come?" asked Isaac.

"To offer a sacrifice."

"And so, we brought wood. What of the lamb?"

Abraham moved on in silence. Uneasily, Isaac glanced back, wondering why his question remained unanswered.

Faith! Faith is believing what I cannot see for the future. I will see my son again, here or when I have joined my fathers in their graves. But now, his every movement is tearing the muscles binding my heart in my chest, my eyes in their sockets. I can't get enough of him.

Isaac secured the bridle of the donkey to a low tree and moved back to loosen the pack. Abraham helped his son adjust the wood on his back. Slowly they climbed the last yards to the summit. Isaac glanced around.

"There seems to be plenty of rock to build a small altar." After dropping the wood, he picked up a rock with two hands and staggered forward to place it on the edge of a small indentation on the summit. Quickly, he gathered several more, placing them to form a rough foundation. He glanced back at Abraham.

"Am I doing this right?"

Abraham nodded wordlessly, as he stopped to study the view from the peak. He stood watching a raven ride the wind currents. The bird's wings shifted slightly and the dark form soared. Below the bird, shadows flowed across the mountainside. Whole sections of the landscape were dark, while other areas shone brilliantly, causing Abraham's eyes to squint against the glare. He could pick out each tree, silhouetted against the ground, the shadow of the tree marking its presence against the tawny rock at its base.

He could stand there all day but he knew he had not come to marvel at the view of this high point. He was there to serve his God. Heaving a deep sigh, he turned to study the ground at his feet, to heft a rock onto the altar. Isaac stepped forward, placing another rock alongside the one his father had set in place. Together, they worked to form the base of an altar.

As Isaac straightened, Abraham seized him by the forearms.

"I am so very proud of you. I don't say that often but you have been the utmost joy of our lives. Each day, we cannot believe we could be any happier, and then, when the sun rises again, you are there, bringing us more joy than we could ever hope."

His voice caught and he seemed to collapse against the young man. Isaac quickly braced himself to take the weight of his aging father. Abraham seemed to have shrunk to mere skin covering his bony frame. Wrapping one arm beneath his father's armpits, he half-carried him to a ledge that extended out of the earth. Slowly Issac lowered him, waiting till his father seemed able to support himself, seated on the rock.

"Rest here!" insisted the young man. "I'll finish the work. This journey has drained you."

Again, Abraham's eyes followed the progress of the stone altar as it rose from the ground, Isaac placing each stone to nestle solidly into the crevices created by the rocks below. One layer, two, finally three layers lifted the upper surface of the altar above the ground.

"Enough!" said Abraham. "We have enough."

Isaac turned and walked back to his father's side, seating himself on the ledge.

"All your life you have heard me speak of this God I worship. The one who called me out of Ur, the one who brought me to this land, caught between the edge of the Great Sea and that muddy stream the local people call a river."

Abraham lapsed into silence, looking out over the hills below their wind-swept perch. Isaac waited for his father to continue and the old man seemed to draw the strength from deep within, breathing out each word.

"This God requires absolute devotion. No other gods can stand before him. I have seen his power in Egypt and the valley of the Salt Sea. By faith I believed that he would fulfill his promise of a son, and you came to your mother and me when we were past the age of childbearing."

"Now he would test that devotion. It seems the fulfillment of his promises requires a further demonstration of faith. He calls for a sacrifice. And if I am to believe, then I must give life to that faith."

"But father, where is the lamb?" asked Isaac.

"God will provide the sacrifice."

They sat as the wind increased, an eery whistle sweeping through the hills and up the summit to the ledge they occupied. Abraham shivered.

"I must believe that God's promise will live beyond my years, no matter what he asks of me.

Slowly, he reached over and grasped one of his son's hands. Gently he traced the tendons across the back of the hand as if memorizing the taut tissue of each rigid line. Drawing out a strip of rawhide, he slowly bound his son's wrist. Isaac's eyes rose from the rawhide and looked deep into his father's eyes. In that moment, he understood the grief that had haunted Abraham as he rode north along the trail.

Abraham looked at him, not speaking and waited. Slowly, Isaac brought his other hand forward, extending it to his father. He knew he could easily overpower the old man.

Abraham, his hand trembling, wrapped the rawhide around his son's second wrist and pulled the leather strip tight.

"Oh, God!" he breathed, "not my son!"

By Faith
Genesis 22:10-14

Abraham collapsed, weeping, bent over his son's hands. His son leaned forward, sheltering the old man with own body.

"My son, I do not understand." Abraham sobbed. "But in all my love, all my pride, I cannot hold back the hand of God. He asks for your life and I could refuse him only to our own destruction. Where can we go that we could hide from his presence? How could I hide you from him?"

"Only by faith can I believe that his promise of your life will come again. He fulfilled his promise once. He can fulfill it again."

The silence from the young man drew Abraham deeper into despair.

"How can I believe? How can I go forward?" he cried.

Both son and father were crying now, clutching each other as the wind seemed to tear at their clothing, their hair.

A raucous cry pulled at the grief of both men. Abraham turned his gaze outward, toward a large raven strutting across the rocky summit toward the men. With a cry, Abraham seized a rock and flung it at the bird.

"No! He is not yours. You will not have him."

The scavenger scuttled sideways, his wings lifting his body inches off the ground. He settled and studied them once again, inching closer.

Abraham seized his son's head in his hands, peering into his face.

"Isaac, I love you."

Isaac gazed back, unable to utter a word against his father, the man who had loved him decades before he had been conceived. Silently, they sat, clutching each other, unwilling to part.

The wind pushed a cloud across the sun, laying its shadow across the peak. Abraham shivered and Isaac drew back slightly to look down at his father. The old man's face remained damp from the tears. He looked up at Isaac. Unspoken, each knew the role of the sacrifice to be performed on the windswept peak.

First the rocks, then the wood. Abraham helped his son climb onto the wood. He lay there, looking at his father. Isaac, knowing the truth of what God was asking, shut his mind to the brevity of the next moment.

Abraham pulled the knife from a sheath at his side, his eyes never leaving his son. He placed the knife on the altar next to the young man, bound in rawhide. Slowly, the old man sank to his knees, arms stretched out to grasp his son's head and hands with each of his own hands.

"God, where can we go to hide from you? I cannot save his life if you stretch out your hand to take it. You have promised and I believe."

A deep sob issued from the old man but he rose, gripping the stones, to face his son. He seized the knife and raised the blade to his son's throat.

Isaac's dark eyes bore into his father's soul. He lay there waiting, not flinching as the sharp edge of the stone knife came to rest against the throbbing artery in his neck.

"Abraham!" A harsh voice tore through the shadows that stretched from the thorny bushes that lined one sloping edge of the summit. Abraham's head jerked back, his fingers lost their hold, the knife clattering to the rocks at his feet. His fingers were frozen into a claw, as a mighty force refused to release them. His arm remained frozen at his side.

Grasping the edge of the altar, he turned to look. Who had called? He peered at the brush, seeing no one. Again, the voice spoke.

"Abraham! Do not harm the boy. I know that you fear God for you have offered your son, your only son to me."

Abraham sank to the ground, shaking. He gasped for breath as if emerging from deep under water.

A low protest rose from the brush beyond the altar. Abraham peered into the shadows of the brush, where the form of a goat seemed caught in the tangle. Uneasily, the goat shifted, straining to pull the coil of its horns from the brush.

Bewildered, Abraham stared at the goat. He was certain the animal had not been there moments earlier. He was certain nothing living had stirred on that peak other than himself, his son and one black raven. Yet, here was the sacrifice caught in the tangle of brush.

With a harsh cry, he flung himself onto his son. Wrapping his arms around the young man, he raised Isaac's shoulders, rocking back and forth as if comforting a small child. Harsh sobs broke the stillness, the wind now silent before the presence of the Holy.

"My son!" gasped Abraham. "My son, returned to me from the dead!"

"Abraham!" the voice called, again. "I swear by myself, the Lord, that because you have done this, because you have not held back your only son, I will surely bless you. Your grandchildren will multiply until they number as many as the stars over your head. Your descendants will conquer this land and live in the cities of their enemies. They will bless all the nations of the earth because of your obedience."*

Abraham stared down at Isaac, slowly running his thumb through the tears that brimmed and overflowed in his son's eyes. Isaac raised his hands to his father, as if in supplication.

Startled, Abraham seemed to glimpse the bonds for the first time. He fumbled for the knife, running it through the rawhide to set his son free.

Abraham shuddered as the strips fell away. He grasped his son, holding him tightly. Isaac wrapped his arms around his father's waist, clutching his garments. Abraham could feel the muscles of his son's arms, tighten around him. The tendons tightening, muscles flexing. He would never forget the feel of those arms around his waist!

* Genesis 22:15-18

He looked down into Isaac's face. The sun sparkled off the tears below his son's eyes, light glancing off his teeth gleaming in the smile. Drawing the face into his shoulder, Abraham moaned.

"Alive. You have come back from the dark, the cold earth. No longer dead. You are alive!" *

The servants, watching from the hills below, wondered what could hold their master and his son.

"Look," one called. "I see the smoke. The sacrifice has been made."

The other nodded in agreement.

"The atonement has been made."

---

* Hebrews 11:19

More Questions

This is a difficult story to read and understand. Any parent would question why God would ask them to take the life of their child.

What is your perception of God?

Why did God ask Abraham to trust him?

Can you define the word *trust* in your own words without resorting to the dictionary?

When have you taken a step of faith without seeing what lay ahead?

Take a moment to re-write I Corinthians 13:12 in your own words.

Part III

*The lesson is one of trust.
The decision is to trust God
when we cannot understand
what he asks of us. The
decision to trust him when it
seems beyond all reason.*

The Lessons We Must Learn

Why did I tell you the story of Abraham preparing to sacrifice his son? I do not equate God's call to Abraham to sacrifice his son as equal to my own loss.

The lesson is one of trust. The decision to trust God when we cannot understand what he asks of us. The decison to trust him when it seems beyond all reason. To this day, many parents, when learning of the death of our son, shake their heads.

"I don't know how you do it," they tell us.

As we work through the loss of a loved one, in time all the uproar is reduced to a distant murmur and you are left to quietly grieve. One man who lost both his sons within a span of two years to a degenerative condition, told us, "You will be driving down the street one day, and for no reason, suddenly you will find yourself crying, tears rolling down your face. You're doing well but it just hits you now and then, unexpectedly."

Ecclesiastes talks about a time to grieve. As the initial shock passed and the is funeral over, we looked forward to life returning to a familiar pattern. We wanted the time to grieve without being on the public stage. Ken and I had lost our beloved son, one whom we had desired, reared and nutured as he grew into a mature adult. There were times, when a memory would reduce us to tears. We spoke freely of Marty to each other and to those who came through our lives. We kept the grieving private.

As I think back on the time after our son was killed I am struck by one thought.

God is good.

A mocking voice calls out, "Good? This God has taken your beloved son. How can you say he is good?"

When tragedy strikes or our fortunes diminish, many Christians fall back on the verse found in Romans 8:28.

"For we know that in all things God works for the good of those who love him, who have been called according to his purpose."

For someone standing outside the Christian faith, this verse may seem a bit jaundiced. How can one say that in the grief of losing a child, God works all things for good? This is a difficult question to answer. In the days, the months and years that followed, we watched as God worked in the details of preparing for a funeral and in our interaction with other people. God was present.

Years later, as we gained some perspective, we could see the good that was mingled with our loss like strands in a tapestry, some dark, some light. The end result was one that emphasized God's love and provision. When faced with such deep grief, we had to rely on God to know the bigger picture where he works all things for good. We recognize that God loves us. He uses the difficulties, the tragedies that come into our lives to shape and mold us into the people that reflect his character. Ultimately, we do not see the effect of isolated incidents but rather we witness the sum total of our life that is so much more than a single event.

Saying God is good may seem to diminish the loss of a child, a child we wanted and loved so deeply. Yet throughout the process, we recognized that God was the one who gave us this gift of a son. In turn, God was the one who could take his life. I did not spend much time considering those who had actually planted the explosive device (IED) or the man who had thumbed the remote control. They were inconsequential. I understood that it was God who had chosen the number of days Marty would live and knew the time of his death.

In those first moments, as I saw the Marines approach my front door, I knew what was coming. God, in his mercy, did not leave me alone to deal with this loss. Instead, he directed Ken to come home early that day and we faced that news together. God is good. Even when our lives took an unexpected turn, he was there to give us what we need. And in our loss, I recognized that provision.

Perhaps one of the hardest tasks following the Marines' notification of our son's death was to tell our family members, starting with our daughters and our parents. One daughter began to scream, her body rigid. Our other daughter took the news more calmly, only to break down months later, sobbing on a beach, alone. Our parents cried and grieved.

The pastors of our church, with the senior pastor's wife and a friend, showed up unannounced at our home that evening, to pray with us and to listen to our account of what had happened. I stepped away to answer a phone call from one of Marty's friends. I asked her to pull over as she was driving and told her that Marty had been killed earlier that day. Her wails echoed over the phone and I began to pray with her, to remind her that he was not so much gone as removed from our lives temporarily.

As I spoke, seeking to comfort her, my friend placed her hand on my shoulder to grant me her strength. I realized I was comforting a young woman who should be seeking to comfort me. This seemed so strange and it would happen repeatedly over the next few days. Most callers haltingly spoke their condolences but one acquaintance identified himself and then said nothing. The moment stretched long and to fill the silence I began to share my faith.

A contractor was building a garage and apartment on our property. The next day, when he arrived, we explained what had happened. He offered to suspend work for a few days but we insisted that he continue. Normalcy gave us a touchstone as our lives shifted off course. We chose to go to work that morning and told an employee and a couple of clients what had happened.

Two friends arrived at our office with a large tray of

meat and cheese to feed our extended family that would arrive. As we talked, the phone rang and a man explained that he was looking for the right shop to help him complete a project. I assured him that we made every effort to satisfy our customers. But he would not be assured, he kept demanding to know whether we could do the job to his satisfaction. The minutes stretched on. One friend was ready to grab the phone and get rid of this obnoxious individual. I patiently worked with the man but couldn't help wondering if this was some sort of harassment.* I finally explained that I had done all I could to satisfy him on the phone. He would have to come into the shop. God's presence had given me the ability to deal with this difficult person.

When I returned home, I walked through the front door to find a woman I did not know in my house. One of the sub contractors had insisted his wife come over and help with cleaning, laundry and meals. This woman did not exude a warm, sympathetic approach. She watched me, unsmiling, seeming to take offense at my surprise. How very awkward! I fled into my bedroom, shutting the door and sat on my bed, shutting the door behind me. Glancing over, I realized she had been in this room, digging the dirty clothes out of the hamper in my closet. I felt as if my privacy had been invaded even as I sternly lectured myself to be grateful for the help. I pleaded with God for a gracious attitude.

The phone began to ring. I watched as three, four more

---

* At the time, the conflict in Iraq was controversial, dividing the populace of our town. The more liberal faction often expressed their dissent in a confrontational manner.

calls came in while I spoke with the first caller. This continued throughout the day, the phone constantly busy. We were inundated with people who wanted to extend condolences.

As Sunday came, I knew I wanted to be in church. I wanted to sit quietly and listen to the music and God's word. We arrived a couple minutes late, slipping into our seats. I watched as awareness of our presence spread through the congregation. In turn, I became aware of the songs chosen by the worship leader.

"I cast all my cares upon you." he sang. "I lay all of my burdens down at your feet. And anytime I don't know what to do, I cast all my cares upon you."

"You are my hiding place. You fill my heart with songs of deliverance. Whenever I am afraid, I will trust in you."

I glanced around and realized other members were wiping their eyes. They were grieving with us. As Sunday morning faded into the afternoon, I asked Ken if we could go for a drive just to get away from the incessant phone calls. I needed to breathe fresh air but a blizzard was blowing in. We drove north of town to a small parking area and walked out onto the prairie, stinging pellets of snow driving into our faces. I welcomed the cold, the sting as a gift from God's hand even as I escaped the oppressiveness of voices calling up grief.

In the days that followed, I realized that the church

could not possibly hold the number of people who wished to attend the service. I did not want to hold it at the convention center in town. Our church represented the faith we held at the center of our lives and this was our message to the community. We had placed our faith in God. He is sovereign and will not abandon us in our grief.

I called the church with my concerns and learned that the men were already working to place a video feed in an annex to the sanctuary. The women were baking cookies and preparing sandwiches for those who would attend. All of these incidents demonstrated God's grace working But most important, we could feel the prayers of others lifting us, carrying us through that difficult week. Our friends were there to grieve with us, to provide for our physical needs, to listen if we needed to grieve aloud. This was not something that just happened. It was due to the relationships that we had developed over time. God was providing for us through his people.

As I later reflected on the loss of our son, I could see that God had not left us unprepared for this difficult time. I had been raised as the child of protestant missionaries living in the jungles of Ecuador. Death was a very real element in our lives, whether as a result of a tragic accident, a snake bite, a plane crash or some other cause. We lived with the reality of death as it came to friends and those living near the station. As I grew older, I began to see God's hand in preserving my own life.

For Ken, growing up in a small mining town, accidents were part of his life as well. There was the very real danger that men could be killed as they went to work in the mines each day. He had worked 2,000 feet under the earth's surface, listening to the timbers popping under the weight of the rock surrounding the miners. Later, during the years when our country fought a war in Vietnam, Ken served in the Navy. He understood the purpose of the training they had received.

Both Ken and I could look back at our lives and the experience we had gained through previous difficulties and some unusual incidents. In the years after we married, we had struggled financially and experienced God's provision for us. Our early years were preparation at God's hands for what was to come. With each incident, we learned to trust God a little more. In taking small steps with God, we learned that we would come through difficult circumstances and survive to be happy and blessed.

In the weeks after Marty's death, I had several women tell me that they could never handle the loss of one of their children. Recalling my own struggle with God, I would ask, "If this is what God chooses, how will you stop him?"

We often quoted a passage from the book of Job, blending two verses together:

"Shall we accept good from God, and not trouble?
The Lord gave and the Lord has taken away;
Blessed be the name of the Lord; may his name
be praised."

We all need time to review how he has led us, how he

prepared us through previous difficulties and taught us to rely on him so that we can face the future with confidence. I began to remind people that God prepares us for whatever is to come. He does not forsake us.

In saying that, I do not believe that God enjoys seeing us in pain. God, in his own timing, prepares us to accept and deal with the progression of life and death, pain and joy. We learn far more through pain than through joy.

As others observed this effort to trust God and to live in his grace, they marveled at how strong we were in our faith. Ken and I shook our heads, knowing the moments when we crumpled behind closed doors. In rising to the challenge from those who questioned how we could live with the loss of our son, I reminded others that it was not my strength they were witnessing but the strength of God that bore us through that difficult time.

These were the lessons we learned in the days following Marty's death. Unfortunately, the pace of life was hectic and we responded by trying to run a little faster. We had a friend who quietly stood back and watched, biding her time. She had lost her husband years earlier. She knew some of what was required from us. One Sunday at church she came up and handed me a small pamphlet by Elizabeth Elliot. She stated that this had been a big help to her.

Growing up in Ecuador, I had lived with the children of four of the five men who were killed by the Waodani (Auca) people. Elizabeth (Betty) Elliot was the widow of Jim Eilliot, one of these men. With this in my background, days later, I turned to her words.

She recommends six steps as we move through the grieving process.

First, we must be quiet. We must stand still and acknowledge that God is who he says and that he is sovereign.

Second, we give thanks. We thank God for the one he has given us. We thank God for the time we had and we thank him for knowing what is best for that individual.

Third, we must avoid self pity. When self pity comes knocking, we change our thought patterns. We again give thanks and look to God for his provision.

Fourth, we accept that loneliness follows a loss. This is natural. God calls us to depend on him in our loneliness. He wants to fill the empty spaces. We offer him our loneliness and ask him to fill that lonely place.

Fifth. Offer that loss to God as a gift. I chose to offer my son and my grief back to God.

And the final phase, we step outside of our grief to do something for others.

Allow me to explain how we practiced each of these points in the months that followed.

For me the idea that we must be quiet and wait on God was not a new concept. I had noticed that one of the common elements among the women who lost sons and daughters in Iraq is a tendency to throw ourselves into a whirlwind of activity after the loss. That may be true of other people as well. Somehow, it allows us to feel as if we are in control in the face of a grief that had been inflicted on us. For all I've said about trusting God, the whirlwind in that first week swept me away from time to sit quietly and listen to the One who is in control. Once again, God began to remind me that I needed to take the time to slow down, to breathe, to allow time for him and to absorb all that had happened.

In being still before God, we have to recognize that he is sovereign over all things, all people. I believed then, and still do, that God is in control of all things. I do not believe that he sits back and watches events unfold on earth and then tries to manipulate them to our benefit. As a consequence of that belief, I had to accept that God knew an IED would take Marty's life. I could choose to scream at God for taking my son or I could sit still and learn who God was, who God is and who he will be.

As we come to see more of God, I find it amazing that in his righteousness, God tolerates men and our arrogant disregard for him. God has not swept us all from the earth in anger over our disobedience to him. He shows grace and mercy every day in the little acts of living, in the larger acts of survival. It is humbling to stand in the presence of an Almighty God and address him as my Father.

Like me, Ken was working through his own understanding of God's sovereignty. In the mornings, he would walk along the hill behind our house, watching the sunrise spread from the mountains on the edge of town into the neighborhood. He watched the wind stir the trees along the hillside, the tiny hummingbirds racing to each flower, sucking down the nectar that nourished their frenzied flight. He understood that God had promised to care for each sparrow but what of our son?

A passage in Isaiah 40 touched him deeply as he walked through the grass on the hillside. The chapter begin, "Comfort, comfort my people, says the Lord."

Then the prophet, Isaiah writes,

"A voice says, "Cry out."
And I said, "What shall I cry?"
"All men are like grass, and all their glory is like the flowers of the field. The grass withers and the flowers fall, because the breath of the Lord blows on them. Surely the people are grass. The grass withers and flowers fall but the word of our God stands forever."   Isaiah 40:6-8

Ken frequently cited this passage for others. I struggled to understand how he found the passage comforting as he compared man to a flower that flourishes for a day and then is gone. Yes, my son was gone. How was this comforting? For years, we had both admired the wild flowers that bloomed across the rocky hillsides. We had seen the grass grow in the early spring, only to turn rasping dry by late fall. He understood that the grass and flowers lived only for a season, fragile under the harsh sun, susceptible to killing frosts.

Before the eternal God, we are fragile. We might be taken in an auto accident or swept away by the ravages of disease. The breath of God can blow us into oblivion.

The passage in Isaiah 40 is reminds us that the word of our God stands forever. When all that surrounds us is shifting, we can rely on God's promise to be faithful to us.

In our weakness, in our grief, he does not forget us. God promises to give us his strength. He stands ready to walk with us, to hold us when we crumple under the difficulties we face in life. He is always present. He never fails. His word stands forever. He keeps his promises. Even when our world seems to cave in, God's strength is what holds us up, allowing us to go forward. He doesn't let go when we reach out to him, just as I had asked when confronted by the news of Marty's death.

The last verse of Isaiah 40 assures us we are borne up and onward on eagle's wings, a reference to God's provision.

> *"But those who wait on the Lord will renew their strength.*
> *They will soar on wings like eagles;*
> *They will run and not grow weary,*
> *They will walk and not be faint."* Isaiah 40:31

This promise is our source of comfort. In working though his own grief and knowing his own weakness Ken worked to understand what God was doing in our lives. He understood that his strength came from God. We each had to turn to God, to rely on his promise, if we were to rise and walk again. This is only possible when we have a relationship with him. We are called to wait on God.

For six months, Ken working through his understanding of God's sovereignty in Marty's death and the greater picture of God's work in our lives. He shared his thoughts with others, trying to explain how contemplating God's mighty power, demonstrated in creation around us, had deepened his faith. He spoke of his observations in the way a dove's foot would grasp a branch, of how the tiny hummingbirds would fly backward and dart at sharp angles in intense combat. Standing beneath the giant pines on the hillside he recalled that God says the trees clap their hands in praise to him. He thought of the wind which no one can see and yet the wind swept through the trees as a song of praise. He was truly learning to be still before God, growing in his understanding of God's sovereignty.

When we take the time to consider God's sovereignty and his grace toward us, we are led to be thankful. Thanksgiving overflows, swamping our lives with the knowledge of God in every breath. In the midst of grief, this can be quite a task. But thankfulness flows out of us as a gift to our creator, to the one who sustains us and who, in his timing, claims our mortal lives. Those who fail to understand this position may choose to roar at God, demanding to see his presence in their lives. But in giving thanks, we are lifted beyond grief, beyond our momentary circumstances to look at the one who made us. We may still shed tears, but we are linked to a life-giving hope.

As the weeks crept by, that sense of thankfulness took on an unexpected revelation. I suddenly realized that in grieving my son, I had given little thought to the men who had planted the IED that took Marty's life. When you credit God as the one who sustains life, there isn't much room for blaming others. Earlier, I had mentioned Lt. Carey Cash's book that had described the ambush directed at 1/5 Alpha, Marty's company. As I contemplated Marty's death, I was reminded of how God had chosen to protect Marty and the other men of that company. He had turned aside bullets and rocket-propelled grenades. I was reminded that Marty had raced through enemy fire to save his comrades and yet God had not spared his life when the IED had exploded.

It would have been so simple for God to reach out and turn aside the shrapnel that penetrated my son's brain. It would have been so easy to sink into self pity and anger at the men who planted that IED. I saw other Gold Star moms struggling with self pity. They had lost the one they treasured, the one they spent years raising.

After the funeral, one man exclaimed his amazement over the lack of anger expressed at Marty's funeral. He wondered at our insistence in looking to God rather than brewing an insatiable anger toward the men who planted the IED. When we are focused on the sovereign God, we have no room for anger, no room for self pity. We choose to place our focus on the God who spoke the universe into existence. Such a line of thought frees us from despair, from self-pity. We can breath and we can live without such a heavy weight laid on us as we look to the one who gives us comfort and hope.

While I would not describe the loss of Marty as loneliness, many memories come back to me as I drive around town. People recalled incidents with us, sometimes laughing, sometimes tearful. If I had given in to grief, I might have felt overcome by those memories. Instead, I was left with a quiet sense of pride in my son and thankfulness for the years we had Marty in our lives.

I understand that for some who lose a loved one, loneliness and loss can be overwhelming. There are times when I asked God to tell Marty that I was thinking of him, that I loved him. This must be enough. To go further would drag us down into despair. And so, Betty Elliot recommends that we let go of the loneliness. I don't recommend filling the time with a mindless whirl of activity to deaden the pain. Instead, I began to choose my activities carefully, thinking about what was truly important.

I recall the man who told us that we would be driving down the road and suddenly find tears streaming down our faces. What do we do with tears? Other than an expression of grief, what good do they serve?

I would suggest that the tears represent the cost of the gift we offer up to God. They express our deepest sentiments as we struggle with the loss of a child. We offer that child back to God with the tears of grief and thankfulness as a gift, believing God understands our sorrow. They are all we can offer up when confusion and grief threaten to swamp us. God counts every one of those tears, standing with us in our sorrow. While the grief may seem to seep from the deepest corner of our souls, God sees our love for the gift he has given us.

When we consciously release the pain as a gift to God, he transforms our sense of loss into a balm that heals our broken spirits. With that healing, we are able to begin reaching out to others, to offer healing to them. And God, being all powerful, all knowing, makes them his treasure to bless us. This takes the focus off our grief and enhances our time with others. In return, blessing comes back to us.

As the grief diminished, a sense of accomplishment began to replace the sense of loss. We knew we had raised Marty well, in spite of our mistakes. He was not the smartest kid. Yet, we could say that he gave his best, that he stuck to a task till he accomplished his goal. We didn't have the opportunity to watch him grow and come into the fullness of maturity. He did lay a good foundation for that growth. He demonstrated a quiet humility before God and man. He overcame his early limitations and demonstrated that he could set an example for other people that would cause them to strive a little harder to be a little better. As he matured, he practiced the two basic commands in scripture: to love God with all his heart and soul. And then to love others as yourself. He demonstrated his care for others by putting his life on the line when an ambush or firefight broke out. We remain very proud of Marty.

In celebrating what he was, we could move beyond our sense of loss. There were people around us who did not share that outlook. A few who claimed faith crept into our lives, trying to draw us back to our grief, refusing to consider that we might have any other outlook. They disguised their efforts as concern for our well being. In our conversations, I wanted to cry out, "Where is your trust in God? Do you not believe as the Bible teaches that my son is living in the presence of God. If you trust him, why do you concentrate on loss? Why do you drag me down into a pit of grief?"

I had chosen to place my trust in God. I had chosen to believe that God had a better plan for my son. Yes, I missed him but looked forward to the day when we would be united in the presence of God. This is the hope that Jesus gave us in his resurrection from the dead. I wanted to live this belief but these women seemed determined to drag me down and hold me prisoner in the darkness.

These were friends. They meant well but if I could, I turned away every time I saw them coming. With each passing week, I wanted to fight for freedom, for air to breathe God's grace and comfort. I went to the woman who had placed her hand on my shoulder when I comforted one of Marty's friends. This woman had lost her husband in Vietnam. I asked for counsel with my attitude.

I realized that part of my grief was turning into anger and that anger was being inflicted on people who meant well. The friend advised me to set my anger aside and to forgive their lack of trust, their lack of discretion. I was to keep my eyes on God, not on those who wished to keep us grieving. I had grown in living through the loss of my son but that growth was reaching a new stage in dealing with others.

Two questions developed out of this time, as I adjusted to the loss of our son.

If the worse that we could imagine should suddenly break into our lives and if God is in control, did he allow or cause this tragedy to happen? If I believe that God is in control, then the answer is yes, God did allow this to happen. For many people that is just too hard to bear. It is too hard to believe that a God who loves us so deeply would allow us to be so deeply wounded.

And yet, as with the Biblical character of Job, there are times where we must go through very difficult circumstances that threaten to pull us down into despair and disbelief. These are the times when we must examine the foundation of our beliefs.

The second question was equally difficult. Does God love my child more than I do? And, if God loves my child so much, why would he allow him to die so young? As we struggle to come to terms with accepting what God has allowed to happen in our lives, we invariably turn back to the question of whether God loves us. If God loved us, surely he would not ask us to endure pain. I am convinced that he did, and does love my son. The answer to that question lies beyond what we see in our temporal lives. God does indeed love Marty and chose to take him from this earth to live with him. And in return, he offered us comfort.

I could not see the future that awaited my son if God had left him with us. Did an insurmountable trial wait for my son later in life? Did God choose to take Marty before he would be bowed beneath temptation or great evil?

Ken's mother called our attention to Isaiah 57:1-2.

*"The righteous perish, and no one ponders in his heart:
devout men are taken away and no one understands
that the righteous are taken away to be spared from evil."*

It was entirely possible that God, out of his great love for our son chose to take him before great evil could overcome him. I thought about the circumstances he lived in. There certainly was a possibility of great evil in Iraq at the hands of men who were committed to a different god.

The Bible tells us that in the presence of God, there is no sorrow, no evil, no tears. We will know his love and overflowing joy when we stand before God. If this is true, then my desire to see my son restored to us was more about my happiness than Marty! God's love desires the best for another person. Ultimately, Marty was experiencing the best in the presence of God.

Recognizing these two principles, God's sovereignty and God's love for my son, helped me to walk by faith with God. If I cannot see the reason behind what has happened, then I must simply walk in faith, believing that God sees a part of the greater picture that I do not yet see. He knows what my future holds and the reason for what I see as a loss.

My friend's suggestion was wise as I worked at keeping my eyes on God and allowing the Almighty to work with others. As the months passed I became a bit more adept at responding to those who seemed to expect me to be lost in grief. We talked easily about our son, turning aside inappropriate questions.

~~~

Six months after Marty's death, we got a phone call from a friend. One of our former employees, had committed suicide while battling tremendous back pain with potent pain killers. Coming so soon after Marty's death and having talked to this man about our faith, we were devastated. We agreed we should go to the funeral and arrived at the church, feeling a bit despondent. We wondered where this man was to spend eternity. As the pastor spoke about Dale attending his services, we looked at each other in astonishment. Was it possible that Dale had finally come to some sort of faith in God?

After the service, we mingled with the guests at a reception. When we met Dale's sister, she burst out, saying, "I have to tell you about Dale!"

Again, we looked at each, questioning what was to come.

"Thank you for your witness through Marty's funeral," she began. "Dale went to the funeral. He came back and told me that he had started thinking about God. One morning he called me. I was still in my pajamas and he insisted he would come and get me so that we could talk privately at his house."

We nodded, wondering where this story was going.

"He was in tears when we got there," she continued. "He told me that he had been thinking about God and he didn't know if he needed to become a Christian. He was in such grief over the things he had done. He was crying so hard, he could hardly talk.

"Finally, I tried to explain to him that he needed to ask God for forgiveness and he told me he had already done that.

He just couldn't get past his grief over his sins."

We stared at her in amazement. "You mean you're a Christian?" I asked.

"Yes," she said.

Ken and I turned to each other in amazement, big smiles spreading across our faces as the gloom began to lift.

"You're telling us that Dale became a Christian?" I asked.

"Yes! And it started at Marty's funeral. He started to think about God for the first time in his life. Before that, he never wanted anything to do with God."

Ken and I could hardly contain our excitement. We had the assurance that Dale did have an eternity with God. And, we understood that it was because of the witness of our son. So many times I had prayed that at least one person would come to Christ through that witness. I was prepared to never know whether that prayer had been answered, simply believing God for what had happened beyond my personal knowledge.

God, in his goodness, had allowed us a glimpse of one person and his decision to follow Christ. I could not thank God enough for giving me that moment, that assurance that one person was in heaven because of my son. I thought for a moment about Marty and Dale meeting in the presence of God. I thought about Dale clasping Marty's hand, grateful for his witness. At that moment, I could once again say that "God is good."

That moment of exultation did not last. Despite all my

efforts to live above the grief, an intense darkness entered my life three months later.

Confronting Grief

Nine months into the year following Marty's death, grief and darkness began to close in around me. This darkness was more than grief over the loss of Marty. The darkness included anger and doubt. How did I know absolutely for certain that our beliefs were founded in a God that really existed? How did I know that Marty lived on in the presence of this God I could not see. Was I the biggest of fools to be pitied? *

I could no longer escape the questions that haunted me. For someone who has grown up in the church, to question the very existence of God can be unsettling and I was uncomfortable with bringing my doubts to my pastor or any other Christian.

During this time, we watched our neighbor's son come and go from our neighborhood, his life growing ever more bitter with each month. He had become dependent on prescription pain killers and we believed he was addicted to oxycontin that he obtained illegally on the streets. At first we tried to help but we soon realized that he had no intention of breaking the addiction and was merely using us to further his

* I Corinthians 15:17-19

addiction. This was very painful. We had known this young man since he was born. Marty and Payton spent a lot of time together and at one point, Marty had tried to help Payton seek a better path than the one he found on the streets. Watching this young man make such destructive choices, I cried out to God.

"My son was living to the best of his abilities. He had so much to offer and you took him. Yet, you leave this young man who squanders his health and abilities in destructive living. Why did you take a good man and leave such a wreck of narcissistic apathy to continue in the human race?"

Anger began to seep into my soul. I knew God was giving Payton every chance to straighten out his life. Yet, this is a question frequently asked when a good man dies. Why do the righteous die and leave the evil to pursue the destruction of our society?

We continued to turn down his collect calls from inmate holding tanks. The drugs had so disturbed Payton's brain that he could not understand that we were the last people he should call after breaking into our home and stealing various items from us. Somehow he believed that we would pay his bail and allow him the freedom to pursue self destruction. I was discouraged. No matter what I prayed, there seem to be an indifference in him to God's leading.

The questions returned: If God is good, why did he allow Marty to die? Why didn't God protect one of his own? This is an extension of the question I asked previously. Yet it needs to be addressed individually since it goes to the heart of our trust in God.

As both Ken and I struggled to understand God's sovereignty in our grief, we were frequently drawn to the book of Job as are many other people who struggle with this question of why God does not always answer our prayers as we ask.

Job was a wealthy man with ten children. God pointed to Job as an example of a man who was faithful and blameless. Satan, in return, questioned whether Job would be so faithful if his life suddenly seemed to be cursed. God then gave Satan permission to bring great harm to Job without taking his life. First, his cattle and livestock, a measure of wealth, were stolen or killed. Other possessions were damaged, his servants murdered by raiders. Then Job's ten children were killed in a violent wind storm. Finally, Job's health was replaced by illness. In no way did we compare our lives to Job yet we might have asked the same question asked by Job's wife.

"Job, why not curse God?"

Moving on to the New Testament, I was reminded of Peter's boast to Jesus on the eve of the crucifixion. As a disciple of Jesus, he claimed he would follow his teacher through all that might come to try him. Jesus looked at Peter and revealed that Satan had asked for permission to sift Peter as if he were wheat. That thought is enough to chill one's blood when we consider that the great enemy of our souls is hunting us, asking God for permission to rain down destruction on us, hoping that we will deny our faith.

As the challenge deepened, I asked if our faith was based on a fairy tale, if we had placed undue confidence in a God that did not exist. Could I believe this unseen God? Death or great tragedy forces us to examine the existence of God and his relationship to us. How could I prove that what I said about faith did exist in concrete, touchable, seeable evidence? I didn't want to admit my doubt but I had to confront the questions

Of course, I was not the first to ask these questions. To my great relief, I found that the great Christian apologist C. S. Lewis struggled with the same question after the death of his wife, Joy. Eagerly, I turned to his book, A Grief Observed, and failed to find a single concrete thought that I could touch, see or taste. I did discover that this man had come through grief to faith again. If I pursued that same journey, then I might recover my faith.

Take a moment to examine the evidence of the existence of a historical Jesus. Take the time to consider the arguments for his resurrection and then land on the passage from Paul in I Corinthians 15:12-23.

> *But tell me this—since we preach that Christ rose from the dead, why are some of you saying there will be no resurrection of the dead?*

> *For if there is no resurrection of the dead, then Christ has not been raised either. And if Christ has not been raised, then all our preaching is useless, and your faith is useless. And we apostles would all be lying about God—for we have said that God raised Christ from the grave. But that can't be true if there is no resurrection of the dead. And if there is*

no resurrection of the dead, then Christ has not been raised. And if Christ has not been raised, then your faith is useless and you are still guilty of your sins. In that case, all who have died believing in Christ are lost! And if our hope in Christ is only for this life, we are more to be pitied than anyone in the world.

But in fact, Christ has been raised from the dead. He is the first of a great harvest of all who have died. So you see, just as death came into the world through a man, now the resurrection from the dead has begun through another man. Just as everyone dies because we all belong to Adam, every one who belongs to Christ will be given new life. But there is an order to this resurrection: Christ was raised as the first of the harvest; then all who belong to Christ will be raised when he comes back.

Each time the doubts crept in, I reviewed the evidence for the existence of Jesus and the evidence for the resurrection. I claimed the hope that as Jesus rose from the dead, I had hope for existence beyond this life and the belief that I would see my son again, that my hope was not in vain.

Faith is not easy to explain. The answers are not simple. We cannot reach out and touch the reality of what we believe. But that is the substance of faith. *

For Ken, his quiet time on the hill behind our house bore witness to the miracle of God's creation. As I previously mentioned, he watched the sun rise each day, the

---

* Hebrews 11:1-3,6

hummingbirds fly combat missions over the remaining wild flowers. The moisture fell each morning and the trees drew that moisture from the ground, expressed in each slender pine needle. All of creation spoke to Ken of a designer, of a creator who was an omniscient presence in our lives. His thumb-worn Bible spoke the goodness of God to his soul.

"Seeing God as creator is the reason I have never doubted that God was firmly in control," Ken says. "Through creation, he shows me his power, his wisdom and his understanding. The three are irretrievably linked. In every act of God we see these three elements on display and in turn we see God working in our lives. I could see the evidence for God's sovereignty demonstrated in creation and in my life. If he could take such care to design the delicate body of a hummingbird, then I could trust him with the control over my life and the life of my son."

While Ken may have reached a quiet place, I was overwhelmed with many responsibilities. I struggled to make time to sit and read God's word, to contemplate what God was doing as I struggled with grief. No one within our circle of friends guessed at the struggle within my soul. I believed that if I continued to call on God, he would make his presence known in my life. Most likely I would not see him through creation but in the lives of those around us.

A year later I stumbled again. I reviewed the evidence. I reviewed God's goodness to us. But ultimately, my son was gone. I was exhausted, discouraged, struggling with fatigue from a perennial health challenge. My prayers for others seemed to go nowhere, certainly not beyond the ceiling And suddenly, I knew I could not walk by faith; faith was not enough. All of creation was not enough to reinforce my faith against grief and exhaustion.

Such an attitude seems a bit vain when confronted by an omnipresent, all-powerful, all-knowing God. But as God is all knowing, I believed he would understand my frame of mind and gently lead me to a better place. I knelt before him, pleading, "God, I can't walk by faith any longer. I need to see you do something. I need to see you in action. One small thing that will encourage me. Forgive me for my doubt but I just need to see concrete evidence of you working in my life and the lives of others right now."

And then I waited. I wasn't questioning the existence of God or his power. I just told him that I was too weak. I was determined not to grasp at straws. As God began to bring little acts to my attention, I was grateful. Deep down I believed that he had something really good to show me and so I refused to settle for the small moments.

Waiting can be a good place because we don't try to make God into something in our own image. We wait to see all that he is beyond our finite minds. I can not tell you the one thing God did to restore my sense of his presence. One day, I just knew he was there because there had been so many ways he had quietly affirmed his presence in my life.

We can look at death as a final door closing forever on one's life, or we can see it as a portal through which our loved one steps into new possibilities in the presence of God. One choice leaves us in grief, the other resounds with hope. The choice is a matter of faith. And in this moment, we know our choice is to stand before God, placing our trust in him.

I had to acknowledge that God's plan for our lives was much more complex than we can understand. Our time on earth is given to us by God's mercy. All we deserve is God's judgement, yet by God's mercy we live each day. Living with this understanding changes our perspective.

We are overwhelmingly grateful that God calls us into his presence when we pass away on earth because Jesus has paid all the debt we owed. Marty could stand in God's presence because of the price that Jesus had paid. I would see him again someday because of the price that Jesus paid for me.

Gratitude leaves us with one response: "Blessed be the name of the Lord."

Walking by Faith

Several years after Marty's death, I was sitting in church while visiting my parents when the pastor said something interesting that I wished to write down for further contemplation. I didn't want to dig through my purse for the next five minutes looking for a pen. I might lose the thought or miss out on something else.

Looking over, I saw a pen in my father's shirt pocket. I calmly reached over and pulled it out to begin writing. My father never flinched or acknowledged the action. I was reminded that as his beloved daughter, I have special access to his front shirt pocket and to his heart. I can ask him at any time to take a moment to give me his undivided attention because I am his daughter.

Thinking about the story of Abraham, Isaac must have felt that way as he walked with his father to his own execution. Did he know what God had asked? Somehow I don't think he did, at least not until the last few moments. He just walked along, feeling that bond, based on trust, with his dad. He had been invited to go some place special. He reveled in that unique moment, unaware that he was the sacrifice that

Abraham had been called to offer.

In my own experience, I have learned that God may call us to the unexpected, to sacrifice what we love most to his supremacy. Sacrifice requires trust, a belief that God knows his supreme will for us in a way we can never comprehend.

On April 20, 2005, at 5:45 p.m., two Marines came to our door to tell us that our son, Lance Corporal Marty Garth Mortenson, had been killed by an improvised explosive device in Ramadi, Iraq.

In the seconds that followed that announcement, I made the decision once again to trust God in my son's death. This was not a new decision but one that I had made repeatedly in the months prior to that watershed announcement. There were days when I argued, pleading for my son's life. Throughout that time, God challenged me with his sovereignty.

Standing before a sovereign God, one comes face to face with mortality. Stripped bare, I had no way to fight for my son's life, I could only plead with God to spare him. Ultimately, if we are honest in the pursuit of God, surrender of what we love most is inevitable. I had to offer God my son, believing that he knew what was best.

So, when the Marines came to our door, I knew God was waiting to hear me surrender, once again.

Marty struggled with consistency in his walk with God but he believed God's promises. He asked for God's forgiveness. In return, he received God's righteousness, spreading over him, making him righteous in God's sight. As he lived and fought in a very dangerous place, God chose to take him, a righteous man, to spare him from evil. We clung to that belief, choosing to believe that God knew what was best. Many watched us and exclaimed over how strong we were in our faith. They didn't see the tears of grief we wept in private. They certainly didn't see my struggle with doubt.

Ultimately, I chose to believe that I would see my son again someday, as we will stand together in the presence of God. One day, reading the book of Hebrews, I came across this passage on faith.

> *"Now faith is being sure of what we hope for and certain of what we do not see. This is what the ancients were commended for."*
>
> Hebrews 11:1

The ancients, men like Abraham, were commended. As with many Christians, for me, Abraham was up on a pedestal. After all, in faith, he had left his home. He had negotiated with God for the life of his nephew. He had believed that God would give him a son from which came the Jewish people, and ultimately those who follow Christ. This was the stuff of big faith, unlike my everyday life. The term 'Patriarch' refers to more that the father of a nation, it describes the man who first began to articulate the faith that has been passed down through the generations to us.

Read a little further in Hebrews 11 and we see Abraham credited with believing God, even as he was asked to sacrifice the life of his son. Verse 19 says that "Abraham reasoned that God could raise the dead, and figuratively speaking, he did receive Isaac back from death."

I seemed to remember another verse along that line later in the chapter and I scanned the verses quickly. There it was in verse 35.

"Women received back their dead, raised to life again."

They received back their dead because of God's sovereignty over death, even as they were enduring injustice and torture. They believed God and he honored their faith. Finally, in verse 39, I read the conclusion.

"These were all commended for their faith,
yet none of them received what had been promised.
God had planned something better for us
so that only together with us would they be made perfect."

The light broke through. I was walking in the same path Abraham once trod! Like Abraham, I believed that God could raise my son from the dead. And as in verse 39, I haven't see that resurrection yet. The day will come, when made perfect, I will see my son again because I have believed God for his promise.

Abraham had no prior experience that would give reason to believe that God would raise his son from the dead. He walked by faith, 'certain of what could not be seen.' As I said previously, I had never personally identified with Abraham. He was in a sphere that I could only see from afar. In a sense I had placed him on a pedestal, apart from my everyday problems. But suddenly, I found we had something in common. We had both been asked to trust the sovereign God with the life of a son. Unlike Abraham, I can look to the resurrection of Jesus to understand God's power over death.

Yes, this journey is hard with lots of questions, lots of tears. In our finite minds we struggle to understand a sovereign God. Regardless of whether the test is in the fate of a child or something else, only by faith, will we reach the final destination, in God's presence, and know what we have accomplished.

God gave us the story of Abraham as an example of faith that pleases him. So, as with Abraham, by faith, we take the next step. We choose to believe God's promises and trust him.

"Now faith is being sure of what we hope for and certain of what we do not see. This is what the ancients were commended for. By faith we understand that the universe was formed at God's command, so that what is seen was not made out of what was visible." (vs 1-2)

"All these people were still living by faith, when they died. They did not receive the things promised, they only saw them and welcomed them from a distance. And they admitted they were aliens and strangers on the earth. People who say such things show that they are looking for a country of their own. If they had been thinking of the country they had left, they would have had opportunity to return. Instead, they

were longing for a better country, a heavenly one. Therefore, God was not ashamed to be called their God, for he has prepared a city for them. (vs 13-16)

"These were all commended for their faith, yet none of them received what had been promised. God had planned some thing better for us so that only together with us would they be made perfect." (vs 39-40)   Hebrews 11

More Questions

Before you set this book aside, ask yourself a few more questions.

In what form do you express grief? Do you see later how God used the loss for good in your life?

Look back at Elizabeth Elliot's five points for confronting grief on page 138. Write your own response to each point.

Think of a time when you felt God lifting you out of sorrow and sadness.

Take a moment to thank God for someone you have lost, naming something specific about that person as you pray. Even if the loss involves a miscarriage, thank God that the child is in his care and that you will meet again one day.

If your perspective on loss has changed, how will you speak to others in the future about the loss of someone they love?

www.ingramcontent.com/pod-product-compliance
Lightning Source LLC
Chambersburg PA
CBHW070428010526
44118CB00014B/1946